Some of the sharpe doing grassroots ministry in eastern nations. As their countries cannot afford specialist writers, their insights are often lost to the church worldwide. This is a shame because the church would be greatly enriched by their insights.

I am so glad for this book, which is introducing to a wider audience the thinking and experiences of some of our outstanding leaders.

AJITH FERNANDO, *Teaching Director, Youth for Christ, Sri Lanka*

❀

Seldom is the Eastern leadership voice, especially of church leaders, heard. This book is a refreshing departure from the usual.

Many themes run through this book, offering a reality from the grassroots of church leadership. It is a delightful reading of visions, aspirations, dreams, struggles and strivings of leaders of local churches in Asia–a guide for those who want to know the issues of Asian church leadership. I endorse this book as an invitation to journey into the world of pastoral leadership in Asia.

REV. C. B. SAMUEL, *Advisor, Micah Global,*
former CEO, The Evangelical Fellowship of India
Commission on Relief (EFICOR)

In my lifetime, Christianity has become a truly global faith. A few generations ago, Christianity still came mainly from the West to the East. Now, as we become a global Church, it is wonderful to see how our faith impact cultures, peoples, and world views. While we all worship the same Christ, how he is expressed in different places is indeed wonderfully diverse, uniquely creative, and beyond our imagination.

This collection of works from Asia sheds light on how God is experienced in different parts of his world. A perspective from our global brothers and sisters not only enriches our own understanding of God, but encourages us once again to see our unique privilege to be involved in his Great Commission.

EDWIN KEH, *CEO, The Hong Kong Research Institute of Textile and Apparel*

❀

Voices in the public square are to be heard! These men and women model their lives, ministries, and calling in societies across Asia. God gives us a beautiful perspective of how he is forming the Church and societies in this young century.

SAMUEL CHIANG, *CEO, The Seed Company*

Our Lord's global vision promoted through his local voices! This book harnesses the good of her past, connects better leaders among the present, and promotes some of the best voices for the future well-being of Christ's Church.

If one cares to understand, appreciate, and support growing healthier ministry initiatives through local voices, read about what God is doing in the world's most populous, and therefore precious, region. Let's join them in providing a platform to the voices you will hear inside.

RAMESH RICHARD, *President, RREACH/Professor, Dallas Theological Seminary; Founder, Trainers of Pastors International Coalition [TOPIC]*

❃

Testimony builds faith. Reflection develops depth. Here's a delightful compilation of testimonies and reflections, from different Asian Christian leaders, to build faith and develop depth. I've enjoyed reading it!

EDMUND CHAN, *Leadership Mentor, Covenant EFC; Founder, Global Alliance of Intentional Disciplemaking Churches*

You need to read these chapters–every one of them. Grow what you know about Christians in eastern countries. Rethink what you thought you knew. Listen to these new voices. Study their approaches. Learn from God-followers who are presenting original culturally-appropriate ways to bring Jesus to their countries.

MARLENE LeFEVER, *author of* Creative Teaching Methods
and architect of two survival curriculums,
Ebola Crises *and* After the Earthquake

❀

It's my privilege to commend *Eastern Voices* to Christian leaders and enterprises focusing in the Far East. These are the voices of practitioner-scholars who are reflecting on numerous areas of kingdom advance in the Church. There is wisdom here and people like me, born and bred in the West, are in sore need of this wisdom.

LON ALLISON, *Pastor of Teaching & Outreach,*
Wheaton Bible Church

The challenge of Asia is immense, with an estimated 60% of the entire world living there, including two countries whose populations together approaches 2.5 billion souls. The context of Asia is complicated, diverse, and spiritually overwhelming, with most of the world's Hindus, Buddhists, and Moslems living there–plus more than a billion whose world view is classified as secular. These realities make *Eastern Voices* an answer to an urgent need–to understand ministry in Asia through the eyes and wisdom of Asian leaders.

Eastern Voices takes us into the classroom of experienced, godly Christian leaders as they address issues that we in the Western world might not understand. This first of many anticipated volumes is a library of training for people serving in Asia.

The book asks the question, "Can you hear the voices?" I strongly encourage any Christian leader interested in or burdened for Asia to sit, read *Eastern Voices*, and listen carefully.

PAUL BORTHWICK, *Development Associates International, author of* Western Christians in Global Mission: What's the Role of the North American Church

One of the most profound evidences of our being made in the image of God is the hearing and the telling of our stories. The God of Scripture is a story-telling God who has made people to be and do likewise. Many things can keep our story-circles too small, however, and then we fail to benefit from the depth and breadth of what God is doing around the world.

Eastern Voices Volume 1 will help to change that. To hear these particular Christian voices from various parts of Asia is a richly formative gift. The events and experiences are important, but even more important is the chance to hear the Holy Spirit's work inside these varied cultural and personal contexts. We can be awakened beyond the limits of our own daily setting to a fresh awareness of God's faithfulness in different contexts and lives.

What a treasure house. Hear these stories and be moved!

MARK LABBERTON, *President, Fuller Theological Seminary*

EASTERN VOICES

VOLUME ONE

EASTERN VOICES

VOLUME ONE

**Insight, Perspective, and Vision
from Kingdom Leaders in Asia
In Their Own Words**

COMPILED BY ASIAN ACCESS

Asian*Access*
DEVELOP. MULTIPLY. TRANSFORM.

Asian Access
P.O. Box 3307
Cerritos, CA 90703 USA

Asian Access is an interdenominational evangelical missions agency committed to see a vibrant community of servant leaders with vision, character, and competence leading the church across Asia. You can find out more about Asian Access at www.asianaccess.org.

Cover and Book design: Loren A. Roberts/Hearken Creative

ISBN: 978-0-9986861-0-3

CONTENTS

Acknowledgements

MY APOLOGIES up front in that I know I am going to forget to name some deserving people. To a person, everyone involved with *Eastern Voices* has been encouraging and supportive. At Asian Access, I'm blessed with a team of gifted people who are all in with A2's commitment to *identify and develop the right leaders at the right time through the right process, so they can be released to make the greatest Kingdom impact across Asia*. It's a great ministry and a lot of fun.

Eastern Voices was the brain child of Takeshi Takazawa. For years, he has known that his ministry colleagues in Asia have things to say that would be worth hearing by the greater English-speaking ministry world. It was his vision and drive that brought the concept of *Eastern Voices* into reality. (You can enjoy his personal contribution to the project beginning on page 159.)

Asian Access president Joe Handley caught the vision early on and gave me carte blanche (and the funding) to pursue the project with our Asian Access leaders. His unflagging support for *Eastern Voices* has been a major encouragement.

Jeff Johnston, A2's vice president for advancement and communications, was also an early supporter. He has invested his time and considerable expertise into many aspects of the project, and *Eastern Voices* is much better for his investment.

Loren Roberts leads Hearken Creative Services, providing expertise on all manner of video, print, and other media endeavors. Loren guided *Eastern Voices* through design and production, for which this 20-years-out-of-publishing relic is very grateful. It was Loren who suggested one morning, "What if we title the first book *Eastern Voices Volume 1*, and make this an ongoing series?" Beautiful.

The original plan was that my wife Kyle would be able to travel with me a good portion of the time as we developed contributions for the book. That plan was sidetracked when her father was hit with a major illness in February 2015. She has been unfailingly cheerful and supportive, doing the heavy lifting here at home while I've traipsed around the globe. (And thank God, Mac is doing much better.)

Most of all, I'd like to thank the men and women who have contributed the material for *Eastern Voices Volume 1*. They have been willing to step way outside of their comfort zones and risk putting down their thoughts, perspectives, and experiences in a foreign language–English. It has been a real privilege to walk with them in the journey of creating *Eastern Voices*. We are in their debt.

Noel Becchetti
April 2017

INTRODUCTION
Can you hear the voices?

IT'S TIME TO HEAR the voices.

The voices have actually been with us for years–brothers and sisters whom God has raised up to lead His Church and spread His Gospel in their home countries. Men and women of faith, courage, and vision. They have lived much, seen much, done much, learned much. And they have much to share.

But it has been hard for us to hear the voices. We have had to outgrow previous notions of how, and where, God has been at work. For decades, even centuries, we supposed that the primary drive for the Kingdom of Jesus Christ came from the Western world. While much good was done by many good Western people, we missed the good being done by good people in the East–people from South Asia, Southeast Asia, East Asia, West Asia.

It has been hard to understand the voices. As English became and continued as the global trade language, voices from other heart languages have been drowned out. Our reliance on English as the means for multinational communication has created challenges for our brothers and sisters for whom English is their second, third, or fourth language.

And the voices have been lost in translation. Well-meaning Western brothers and sisters have attempted to share the vision, insights, and perspectives of their Eastern brothers and sisters to the English-speaking world. Often they got it right, but sometimes, what our Eastern brothers and sisters were trying to say was lost in the translation.

Asian Access has been blessed with many dedicated, gifted, and visionary leaders. These men and women have had an impact for the Kingdom in their home countries, throughout Asia, and even worldwide. For quite some time, we have felt that they have things to share that would be of great benefit to all of us in the English-speaking ministry world. Recently, God made it possible for us to share some of those voices with you.

We welcome you to *Eastern Voices Volume 1.* Here you will find contributions from 15 different leaders. Each of these leaders has taken a courageous step–putting their thoughts, perspectives, and experiences into writing, in a language not their own. Writing in one's own heart language is difficult enough, much less taking on the task in a foreign language. I am deeply grateful to each contributor you will find in this volume for their willingness to step out so boldly.

My role as facilitator has been to help each contributor to find and express their voice as faithfully and accurately as possible. This project has given me a rare window into each leader's life, perspective, and heart. It has been an amazing privilege.

Eastern Voices Volume 1 is the result of our collective efforts. My prayer is that you will hear each leader's voice, loud and clear, as you read. Any defects in this volume are solely due to my deficiencies as facilitator.

What I am most excited about is found in our title: *Volume 1*. We believe that this is only the beginning of what will be a growing stream of vision, wisdom, and insight offered by our brothers and sisters from the East (and, I expect, from the South) in the coming years.

God has been raising and continues to raise up leaders called to advance the Kingdom in our changing world. More and more of those leaders are coming from the East. I can't wait to hear from them.

Can you hear the voices?

Noel Becchetti
April 2017

Losing My Face To Find My Soul

An Asian Pastor's Journey from Career to Calling

WESLEY KYAW THURA

"It's done." I said these words to my wife Alma as I walked into our home.

I had just met with my supervisors to inform them that I was resigning my pastorate. After twenty-six years, I was walking away from everything that had defined my life and ministry—youth leader, pastor, denominational leader, member of dozens of church boards, committees, and task forces—and all the titles, position, prestige, and power that went with it. My wife and I were leaving behind salary and security to step out on faith. We were closing the door on a career to open the door to a calling.

What brought us to this crossroads?

FORMATION OF AN ACHIEVER

MY CHILDHOOD WAS, to say the least, dynamic. My twin brother and I were the last two of seven children, born to a Christian mother and Buddhist father. Three days after we were born, my father came to the hospital to demand a divorce from my mother. A lifelong womanizer, my father decided it was time to be free to pursue his other romances without the burden of a wife and family. My mother became the bread-earner for a family of eight.

Life was a struggle, but my mother began to express her Christian faith more freely. She particularly began to plant the seeds of faith within me, every day telling me the stories of Jesus in great detail. She and I grew very close.

Perhaps because of the void we felt without a father, my twin brother and I became high achievers. In school, we won all of the academic prizes. We excelled in sports. And even as young students, we were singled out for leadership roles. We learned quickly that acceptance, respect, and even love were achieved through high performance.

A HORRIFYING END—A TURN TOWARD JESUS

IN 1988, THERE WAS a student uprising in my country. We were pushing for more freedom and democracy from our militaristic, socialist government. I became a leader in the democratic student movement.

Our dreams for a better country came to a horrifying end when the government crushed our demonstrations with deadly force. Seeing friends and colleagues killed before my eyes was devastating. I realized political change was not enough. First, there had to be spiritual transformation–beginning with me.

THE FIRST "CALL": CAREER

Upon becoming a born-again Christian in 1989, I immediately gravitated to ministry. I was active in my church's youth ministry and quickly acquired leadership positions. My ministry efforts seemed to bear good fruit.

Pastors, influential church members, and denominational leaders began to affirm my ministry and leadership gifts. Doors were opened for me to get more involved in denominational ministry. I was approached to attend "by invitation only" special events and training seminars. People began to advise me to attend seminary with the goal of entering the pastorate. All indicators seemed to be pointing me to a successful pastoral ministry.

The pull toward church ministry, and ultimately the pastorate, was a call from God. But I see now that I fundamentally misunderstood what it meant to be called to kingdom ministry. I had interpreted calling as preparation for a career as a denominational pastor.

THEOLOGICAL EDUCATION = CAREER PREPARATION

MY FIRST STEP WAS to pursue a theological education. I enrolled at Methodist Theological Institute. After four years, I received my Bachelor's degree in Biblical and Theological Studies, with highest marks.

There is nothing inherently wrong with theological education. But the education I received emphasized the academic and intellectual components of ministry. In many ways, my theological education was similar to my secular education. While the seminary prepared me well intellectually, little attention was paid to helping me learn how to take care of my soul.

This emphasis on the academic and intellectual reflects educational values we hold dear in Asia. In our secular schools, academic and intellectual achievement is prized–often at the expense of developing the whole person. This imbalance spills into our Christian educational institutions.

We produce high-achieving pastors and church leaders who know all the right theology, but struggle with our pastoral hearts. We high-achieving pastors pursue ministry all out, saving little emotional and relational energy for our spouses and children.

Our evangelism training at MTI was an example. We were taught how to share the gospel by using a booklet. Then, we were assigned to share what we learned. One afternoon, along with another senior student, I went to share Christ with a Chinese gentleman. As we were "sharing the gospel" through the use of the booklet, the gentleman finally said, "This is boring. Can you finish soon? I have many things to do." I was shocked–but I was even more shocked when my colleague answered, "Please sit and listen to the end or I will not pass my exam." With wide eyes, the Chinese gentleman replied, "Is that it? Well, for your exam's sake, please go on to the end." Once we had finished, the man jumped up and vanished!

For my next evangelism assignment, I resolved to be more authentic. I went to a grocery shop run by another Chinese gentleman. I greeted him while he was in the midst of moving big baskets of onions and potatoes with his hired men, so I jumped in and helped them. After we finished the task, the gentleman asked me, "Why are you helping us? You are a theological student, aren't you?" (In Burmese culture, someone doing religious studies is accorded high respect and not expected to do manual labor.) I replied, "Helping you is a way I can show you my love and concern for you and your work."

A smile rose on the man's face. "Have some water and a rest," he said, inviting me to his inner room. We struck up a conversation, and I was able to share the gospel with him—without using the thick booklet!

A few days later, the man visited me at my school and asked if we could talk. We sat together in front of the school building. He began our conversation by referring to our previous encounter. He told me he had felt Jesus' love so much through the encounter that he had decided to accept Jesus as his Savior before he left Yangon for Japan. On the front steps of our school, I prayed for him and he accepted Christ.

Through this encounter, God taught me a lifetime lesson: it is not knowledge that brings people to Jesus, but love.

Knowledge puffs up, but love builds up.
1 Corinthians 8:1b

If I have the gift of prophecy and can fathom all mysteries and
all knowledge, and if I have a faith that can move the mountains,
but have not love, I am nothing.
1 Corinthians 13:2

FROM STRUGGLE TO FAME

FOLLOWING MY THEOLOGICAL education, I entered the pastorate. What astounds me, as I look back on it now, was what I understood a pastoral calling to be. In my mind, calling meant that one day I would become a pastor in a leading church in our denomination, serving for a lifetime under our denomination's umbrella. That's as far as I could imagine. I was approaching my pastoral ministry as a career path.

Early on, my pastoral journey was rougher than I'd anticipated. It was a rocky road of ups and downs, joy mixed with tears. I soon realized that while I had the title of pastor, many of the church members saw me as their employee. Rather than lead the church, they expected me to follow their wishes and preferences. I also learned that there were far more spectators than disciples in the church. Being a people-pleaser by nature, I found myself trying to please everyone rather than trying to lead the church as God had called me.

As the years progressed, I began to receive acknowledgement, recognition, and praise–more, it seemed, than many of my fellow pastors. Along with recognition came perks. I began to accumulate positions of title, power, and prestige.

Eventually, I was appointed pastor to the most prestigious church in my denomination. I had arrived.

EARTHLY SUCCESS...SPIRITUAL DESERT

ON MY PATH TO achievement, I had chosen to play it safe, repeating the same activities and the same ministry patterns, over and over again. It was successful–if "success" is measured by creating a safe, shallow church environment that repeated the same calendar of religious activities, year after year. Rarely did people in search of Jesus darken our doors, and other than our annual Christmas evangelistic outreaches (that quickly cooled after the New Year), our church members showed little interest in venturing out from our comfortable sanctuary to mingle with the unreached. "Success" had been achieved–but at a steep price.

On the outside, everything looked fine. On the inside, however, I was dying. My life was filled with fake smiles, superficial relationships, and an endless string of bureaucratic meetings. I was exhausted, bored, and losing the joy of ministry. My soul was shriveling. And I went on like this for years.

THE PARADIGM SHIFT: ASIAN ACCESS

IN 2003, THINGS began to change. Asian Access (also known as A2) was introduced to me by my denominational leader. I was selected to join the inaugural A2 Myanmar Class.

I brought all of my "weapons" and "armor" (my pastoral position, denominational authority, and titles) to the program. But I was ambushed when Rev. Jim Millard, our teacher, said, "Ministry flows out of our love relationship with God. If that is not right, nothing will be right!"

With those words, a light bulb went on in my mind. *We put position and authority first in our ministry,* I thought, *but A2 encourages us to keep our love relationship with God at first priority. We measure our success with performance; A2 tells us that God measures the quality of our discipleship as success. We focus on building our local empire; A2 challenges us to focus on world mission. We focus on career; A2 inspires us to focus on calling.*

Jesus called them together and said, "You know that the rulers of the Gentiles lord it over them, and their high officials exercise authority over them. Not so with you. Instead, whoever wants to become great among you must be your servant, and whoever wants to be first must be your slave—just as the Son of Man did not come to be served, but to serve, and to give his life as a ransom for many."

Matthew 20:25-28

The radical change in my relationship with Christ, and my beginning to understand what an authentic *call* to ministry really was, turned my world upside down.

CRISIS, MIRACLE, RENEWAL

THEN IN 2004, catastrophe struck. My wife, Alma, was struck down with cancer. After the first two of six scheduled chemotherapy treatments, she was a physical wreck and the prognosis was grim.

Then she did an amazing thing. Stopping the chemotherapy treatment, she stepped out on faith and trusted the Lord to heal her. And God did heal her–completely! She is cancer-free to this day.

After regaining her strength, Alma dedicated herself to sharing with others what Jesus had done for her. She reached out joyfully to anyone and everyone, including trash collectors, house cleaners, and others from the Burmese day-laborer class. In Myanmar, these people rank low in the social order. They are spiritually and culturally Buddhist, and are generally considered to be almost impossible to reach.

But God began to reach these people through Alma. Her ministry grew at a tremendous pace. She believed God was calling her to commit herself full-time to this groundbreaking church-planting, discipleship, and community development work. New Life in Christ was born. (You can read my wife's full story in "No Separation: An Asian Woman's Journey into Pastoral Leadership," p. 61.)

Our lives became a dramatic contrast. There I was, pastor of the most prestigious church in my denomination–yet at a spiritual and ministry dead-end. And there was Alma, reaching more people for Christ than our whole church combined!

Asian Access had already begun to change my world. Then my wife's illness, healing, and plunge into transformational ministry showed me what a real ministry *calling* could look like. God was shining a light onto my path, showing me there was another way. So what was I going to do about it?

THE LAST HURDLE: GIVING UP MY FACE

IN ASIA, HOLDING PRESTIGIOUS office and being bestowed with important titles are powerful icons. Once gained, we do not give these things up easily. This emphasis on positional authority is built into our cultural DNA. It is actually a part of what we know as our *face*. In Myanmar, we have a saying: "All good food goes to the Big Face."

This is just as true in the Christian ministry world as it is in larger society. Pastors and church leaders strive frantically to gain the highest positions, most privileged offices, and most elevated titles. Once gained, these leaders will hold onto their titles and positions to the bitter end—many times with disastrous results for the body of Christ and the cause of the gospel.

By pursuing a career in denominational ministry, I had earned Big Face for myself. I was sought after to attend the important religious meetings, gatherings, and conferences as a VIP guest. I was surrounded by people who knew a relationship with the Big Face (me) could provide them with benefits and advantages. Smiles and cheers surrounded me. People sought my advice. I knew I had very, very Big Face.

As I contemplated breaking out of my spiritual prison–because that is what it was–I realized the most difficult part would be to let go of the titles and offices I had accumulated. I would have to let go of the power, authority, and prestige I had built up over twenty-six years, and go right to the "bottom"–a simple servant of the Lord Jesus. *I would have to give up my face.*

There would be real-life consequences. My phone would stop ringing. Invitations to preach, or to attend major events as an honored guest, would dry up. People I counted as my friends would lose interest in our relationship once I lost my places of prestige. But most of all, *I would lose my face.*

It can be hard for someone outside of my culture to understand what losing face can mean for people who live in a shame/honor culture like we have in Myanmar. It is a massive blow to a person's self-image, self-esteem–literally, one's sense of self. In a culture like ours, *face* can be more important than life itself.

In addition, the impact spreads far beyond any one person. Our culture is a group, or *collective*, culture. Rather than seeing ourselves as free-standing individuals, we are intrinsically interconnected to our families, our ethnic, cultural, and language groups, our vocational groups. We are never an individual–*we are group.*

When I lose my face, the shame of this loss spreads out and affects every group of which I am an integral part–my family, my tribe, my denomination. They suffer the shame as well. (Even as I write these words, I realize how little they communicate the power and hold that *face* has in shame/honor cultures like mine.)

HELP FROM THE WORD OF GOD

AS I STRUGGLED with the implications of my decision, I turned to the Scriptures for guidance. I gained a new appreciation for the apostle Paul–who gave up his title, position, and *face* as a Pharisee to follow Christ's calling–when he said:

> *What is more, I consider everything a loss compared*
> *to the surpassing greatness of knowing Christ Jesus*
> *my Lord, for whose sake I have lost all things. I*
> *consider them rubbish that I may gain Christ.*
>
> *Philippians 3:8*

And I gained a new understanding of these words from the book of Hebrews:

> *Let us throw off everything that hinders and the*
> *sin that so easily entangles, and let us run with*
> *perseverance the race marked out for us.*
>
> *Hebrews 12:1*

Wrestling with these issues made me aware of two things I had to have from the Lord to be able to say "yes" to his call: courage and faith. And I realized how lacking I had been in these two areas, for so many years.

TRANSITION TO TRANSFORMATION

THANK THE LORD, he did provide me with the courage and faith to step away from career and to step toward calling. I resigned my position at the church, my board positions, my denominational titles, my committee memberships, all of it. I have joined Alma in the New Life in Christ ministry and have increased my investment in the work of Asian Access Myanmar and other local and international ministries–all at no salary.

As of this writing, it has been 18 months since Alma and I made our leap of faith. We rely on God daily for our needs such as food, clothing, housing, and our kids' education. But there have been many rich rewards. I now have more time for my wife and family. With more time to spend together, tensions in our family have decreased and the love among us has grown. I can see more what the Lord is doing with my family, uniting us, teaching us to understand, help, and care for one another. Our increased understanding in how to build up our family is helping us to build up God's family: the ministry the Lord has blessed us with through New Life in Christ.

It has taken time for God to detoxify me from old thinking and bad practices. But he has...and in the process, I have regained my spiritual strength. I have new energy with which to move ahead into the calling God has given me–a deep investment into New Life in Christ ministries, and a fresh strategic focus on Asian Access Myanmar.

The joy I had lost has been re-found. I am enjoying a new sense of freedom. Most of all, I have rediscovered the *rest* Jesus promises to us when we live into his calling for our lives. I have a new sense of what it means to be God's true servant–someone who stays where God wants him to stay and does what God wants him to do.

SERVANT LEADERSHIP—A LESSON IN HUMILITY

THIS NEW SENSE of what it means to be God's servant has come with some lessons in humility. As a Burmese man, I would normally never lower myself to do mundane jobs in the house such as washing dishes, cleaning clothes, and mopping the floor. Culturally, it is unthinkable. But God has shown me through his Word that being a good husband, father, and family leader means I must literally serve my family–right down to the nitty-gritty tasks of life.

Then he said to them all: "Whoever wants to be my disciple must deny themselves and take up their cross daily and follow me. For whoever wants to save their life will lose it, but whoever loses their life for me will save it."

Luke 9:23-24

While God is generously providing for our daily needs, we are living on less. God being God, he is using our reduced financial circumstances to create some unique spiritual growth opportunities.

The water situation at our house requires that, except for the monsoon season, I have to get up at 3:00 a.m. to operate an electric water pump. Installing a diesel generator would solve the problem, but we cannot afford one.

For the first several weeks, I sat there feeling sorry for myself. "Why do I have to go without sleep every night?" Then one night, God seemed to say to me, "Don't you see that this is a wonderful opportunity to pray–for your family, your friends, your brothers and sisters in the New Life in Christ churches, your colleagues in Asian Access and their families?" What had seemed like suffering has become a wonderful hour of prayer.[1]

Even with the tighter finances, my family and I have a new understanding of the reality of faith and the generosity of God's grace as we do receive his provision for our daily needs. We also have a new awareness of how God's call to reach the world so often starts as small as a mustard seed, located "nowhere," as "nobodies" reach out to other "nobodies" with the love of our Savior Jesus Christ. God has given my family and me new eyes to see how he has prepared us to break out of the box of "career" to experience his mighty work that stretches far beyond any horizon.

FROM CAREER TO CALLING: THE CHALLENGE CONTINUES

THESE DAYS, I PRAY for God's grace to sustain me as I continue the journey away from the past and toward the future. It is an ongoing challenge to resist the pull of my past, which is so infused in me. How hard it can be to keep making the small, simple steps into the future–into God's call. How strong is the pull of my past!

Alma, our children, and I are all in constant need of the Lord's grace and strength as we move forward in our journey of calling. We do not know what the future holds. Just as the Israelites did after the Exodus, we often struggle with the temptation to return to the safe, familiar slavery we once knew. But we are trusting, day by day, that God, through his exceeding grace, will surely accomplish the dream he implanted in my family and me to reach the whole world–one low-status, Buddhist, impossible-to-reach day laborer at a time.

So we fix our eyes not on what is seen, but on what is unseen, since what is seen is temporary, but what is unseen is eternal.

2 Corinthians 4:18

In the spirit of full disclosure, I must confess that, just as this chapter was being completed, we were able to purchase a diesel generator. I am now getting more sleep while seeking new ways to build up my prayer life.

The Ministry of Business

A Fresh Look at Pastoral Sustainability

Editor's note: Because this leader lives and ministers in a country where repression and persecution of Christians is an issue, we have disguised this leader's identity and location.

"You mean you want me to be like you? You want me to be involved with business, with commerce, with making profit? How can that be spiritual?"

The young minister spoke with passion, a disapproving look on his face. He was coming to me seeking financial assistance. But he was upset at my suggestion that he consider a path similar to my own, one that has combined pastoral ministry with the operation of a for-profit business.

I have heard this accusation many, many times. And I responded to this pastor as I have to everyone who makes this accusation (as at the same time they ask me for monetary support):

"Why are you asking for money from a sinful man?"

THE LONG ROAD TO A DUAL-ROLE MINISTRY

GOD HAS TAKEN ME on quite a journey. Along the way, he has given me a vision for how a minister of the gospel can also operate successfully in the world of business, and how business success can be transformational for effective pastoral ministry.

He has shown me how operating with integrity as a businessperson can be a potent witness for Christ, especially in a country like mine, where corruption is endemic. And he has helped me to learn how to leverage my success in business to multiply ministry tenfold.

But it has been a long and challenging road—one that started very humbly.

STARTING AT THE BOTTOM

I LIVE IN A COUNTRY where the dominant religion is mixed with astrology, animism, and other practices. When a child is born in my country, the parents bring in an astrologer to predict the child's future.

This tradition was to prove dire for me. "This boy is going to kill his father someday," the astrologer predicted (literally, *You are born to eat your father*). In a culture where to be a widow is virtually a death sentence, the choice was easy for my mother. She already had several sons—she had only one husband.

My family considered me a disgrace. I was neglected, underfed, and maltreated. It is quite likely that I would have died had it not been for the care I received from my oldest brother. Fourteen years older than me, he had become a Christ follower. This led to his being kicked out of the family. Having to survive on his own, ostracized from his family and community, he reached out to me with the love of Christ.

At 5½ years old, I was seriously ill and near death. My brother took charge of me, nursed me back to health, and housed and fed me. In addition to caring for me, he began taking me to his church.

One Sunday, an older man approached my brother. "I run a home for children," he told my brother. "I sense that God is telling me to take your brother into my home." For the next several years, I grew up in two successive homes for children run by this man. He became another surrogate father and mentor to me. While I had not yet accepted Jesus into my heart and life, I was growing up in an atmosphere of Christian love and an environment where God was worshiped, the Bible taught, and the Lord's compassion and mercy demonstrated daily. It was only a matter of time before I asked God to take over my life.

ZEAL, VISION—AND A NEW BUSINESS

I WAS A BRAND-NEW, 17-year-old Christ follower. There were immediate, exciting changes in my life. I was excited to share the good news of Jesus with everyone everywhere. Under the guidance of my mentor, I shared gospel tracts, helped to show the Jesus film, and worked among fellow high school students. God began to bless these efforts with fruit, and at the tender age of 19, I planted a church.

But at the same time, I had a strong sense that I needed to face the practical issues of my life. How was I going to survive? How was I going to live? I trusted God, but was quite aware of the lack of capacity in the Christian community. In addition, the culture in my country breeds isolationism. Each person's fate is considered his or her own, and the instinct to help those in need is underdeveloped. So along with the new church, I started a grocery business.

Thus, I was on a simultaneous dual-track learning curve. I was gaining experience in pastoral ministry while at the same time learning how to run a commercial, for-profit business. These dual roles did not create tension for me. After all, didn't God's Word include the Parable of the Talents?

"Again, it will be like a man going on a journey, who called his servants and entrusted his wealth to them. To one he gave five bags of gold, to another two bags, and to another one bag, each according to his ability. Then he went on his journey. The man who had received five bags of gold went at once and put his money to work and gained five bags more. So also, the one with two bags of gold gained two more. But the man who had received one bag went off, dug a hole in the ground and hid his master's money.

"After a long time the master of those servants returned and settled accounts with them. The man who had received five bags of gold brought the other five. 'Master,' he said, 'you entrusted me with five bags of gold. See, I have gained five more.'

"His master replied, 'Well done, good and faithful servant! You have been faithful with a few things; I will put you in charge of many things. Come and share your master's happiness!'

"The man with two bags of gold also came. 'Master,' he said, 'you entrusted me with two bags of gold; see, I have gained two more.'

"His master replied, 'Well done, good and faithful servant! You have been faithful with a few things; I will put you in charge of many things. Come and share your master's happiness!'

"Then the man who had received one bag of gold came. 'Master,' he said, 'I knew that you are a hard man, harvesting where you have not sown and gathering where you have not scattered seed. So I was afraid and went out and hid your gold in the ground. See, here is what belongs to you.'

"His master replied, 'You wicked, lazy servant! So you knew that I harvest where I have not sown and gather where I have not scattered seed? Well then, you should have put my money on deposit with the bankers, so that when I returned I would have received it back with interest.

"'So take the bag of gold from him and give it to the one who has ten bags. For whoever has will be given more, and they will have an abundance. Whoever does not have, even what they have will be taken from them. And throw that worthless servant outside, into the darkness, where there will be weeping and gnashing of teeth.'"

Matthew 25:14-29

Jesus' point seemed clear (and still seems so today). God gives us talents and gifts, including material gifts. He also holds us responsible as to how we use them. Doing nothing with our talents isn't "spiritual" –it's sin.

EDUCATION, EXPERIENCE, AND CHALLENGE

THE NEXT SEVERAL YEARS were a whirlwind of opportunities, experiences, and challenges. I left home for a year of Bible school, then returned to the church. But by then, new leadership had taken over. There was no position for me. Nonetheless, I remained at the church as an unpaid worker. To survive, I took a dishwashing job.

One day, a foreign missionary overheard me singing Christian hymns while I was washing dishes. "I have an opportunity for you," he told me. He took me into his home, giving me a job as gardener, cook, car washer, and general caretaker for the compound.

After two years living and working there, this missionary arranged for me to continue my theological studies at a school in his home country. While it was quite a culture shock from my country, I survived the transition and completed my pastoral training. I also reconnected there with the wonderful woman from my home country who eventually became my wife.

We were finishing our studies, preparing to return to our home country to minister, and considering a life together. Along with our vision for ministry, God kept us mindful of the practical issues we would face, first and foremost, making a living. There was still no Christian infrastructure to speak of in our country. And there was certainly no network of churches that could financially support pastors. We knew we would have to support ourselves.

We began to save every penny we could, living as simply as possible. By the time we graduated and were ready to return home, we had each saved an amount of money.

HOLY INVESTING

IN THE MINISTRY WORLD we were familiar with, the spiritual ethic was to spend all of one's money for the ministry and trust God that he would provide when the funds ran out. But the Holy Spirit had begun to work on me while I was still at school. "Ministry should be sustainable for the long term," I sensed God telling me. "I have provided you with resources. Why don't you invest some of those resources to build the financial ability to maintain and grow your ministry?"

This was a radical idea then, as it is now. In my country, ministers (of any religion) are supposed to be above "worldly" concerns like business, commerce, and finance. Involvement in areas like these are considered of the flesh, something tainted. And there is an expectation that to be truly spiritual, ministers should also be poor.

Yet God continued to give me a vision for how wise investment and management of our resources could be a springboard for ministry growth and vitality. I shared this vision with my future wife. After some time of consideration and prayer, she came into agreement with the vision. She was willing to join me in investing some of her resources into commercial ventures, for the sake of the ministry.

We were not back home very long when we were approached by some local businessmen who had learned we had returned with money. "We are involved in land purchasing and development," they told us. "There is an opportunity that could prove profitable. Would you be willing to invest?"

After research, discussion, and prayer, we did invest. This investment proved to be quite successful. This was the beginning of the land purchase and development business that we run to this day.

BUSINESS SUCCESS, MINISTRY EMPOWERMENT

OVER THE YEARS, God has blessed our business efforts. We search out affordable land that needs work. After purchasing, developing, and making it ready for sale, the parcels we have created from the original block of land are sold, for a profit.

Some of the profits are used to underwrite the many ministries God has also blessed us with. Beginning with a new church plant, God has enabled us to develop a network of churches, both in our capital city and throughout the country. He has also enabled us to build and manage a Bible college, several children's homes, an ongoing ministry to vulnerable elderly men and women, and a rescue home for girls. One recent year, over 60 percent of the budget for these ministries was covered through business profits.

In addition, God has enabled us to use the business to grow churches. In each area we develop, one parcel is reserved for a new church plant. In a country where many obstacles can be raised against the building of Christian churches, our development business gives us a unique open door to grow more churches.

Even more fulfilling is how God has created opportunities for outreach through our business. We live in a country where corruption is endemic. It is assumed that in business, dishonesty and financial manipulation are the norm. We have pledged to the Lord that we will run our business with integrity. Over the years, God has graced us with a reputation for fairness and honesty that is known throughout the community. People want to work with us because they know they will be treated with respect. They can trust that we will not cheat them.

We are often asked, "How can you operate like this when you could make so much more money by cutting corners, like everyone else does?" What a wonderful opportunity to share how our faith in Christ and the values of Jesus enable us to conduct business with integrity, trusting that God will bless our efforts. Our involvement in the business world has provided us with many, many opportunities to witness for Christ and to reach out to others with the Good News of salvation.

CUTTING CRITICISM—AND GOD'S RESPONSE

OUR JOURNEY AS MINISTERS and businesspersons has come at a price. We constantly endure criticism from those who consider any minister involved with something as worldly as business to be tainted. "You are only in it for the money," we are accused. "You just want to get rich at the expense of others."

We try to weather the criticism as graciously as we can, trusting that God will uphold our reputation over the long term. But when possible, we also try to gently point out why we believe our approach actually enhances our spiritual growth and maturity:

- Rather than being constantly dependent on handouts, God has enabled us to create, build, grow, and maintain multiple church, outreach, and compassion ministries.

- In an environment where many worthy ministries tragically die due to lack of resources, God has allowed us to sustain healthy ministries for many decades.

- In our part of the world, Christians are constantly accused, "You are Christian only so you can get money from the West!"

Let me be clear: we raise funds to support our ministries. Our ministry budget is funded through a combination of donations and revenues contributed from business profits. And we are grateful for the financial gifts of generous donors from all over the world. But our ability to continue ministry, even if outside donations were to decrease or dry up completely, strengthens our witness as free-will followers of Jesus Christ.

THE BIG PICTURE: BUSINESS AS MINISTRY

OUR JOURNEY CONTINUES. My wife and I experience successes and setbacks, triumphs and trials. We are on a lifelong journey of learning. But over the last thirty years of ministry and business experience, I believe God has taught us lessons that could empower the larger body of Christ, especially in places where the kind of supportive Christian infrastructure that exists in the West is lacking, and tangible resources are in short supply. In other words, places like where we live.

Here are a few lessons we believe God has taught us:

- God does not divorce the "spiritual" and "material" worlds like we often do. All of creation is his, and he is able to sanctify *all* of his creation–including business, commerce, and finance.

- Business, for the Christ follower, is not something to be avoided, but to be embraced. It can be used for great good.

- Satan has tainted business, commerce, and finance. Through God's power and spirit, we can *redeem* them.

But we also must be aware of dangers that can lie ahead:

- Success can breed pride. We can begin to think that our business efforts are thriving because of our own strength and skills, rather than continually acknowledging that it is God who grants us favor through his grace.

33

- The more of this world's resources we gather, the less dependent we can become upon God's Spirit. Left unchecked, this can be fatal.

THE MINISTRY OF BUSINESS: IS IT FOR ME?

"For I know the plans I have for you," declares the
LORD, "plans to prosper you and not to harm
you, plans to give you hope and a future."

Jeremiah 29:11

MANY YOUNGER MINISTERS ask me, "Should I pursue a dual calling? Should I be involved in both ministry and business?"

Perhaps you are asking the same question. Only God can ultimately provide you with the answer to this question. But while you seek God's guidance, allow me to provide some counsel from my experience:

- Not everyone will be called to a ministry/business dual role.

- Not everyone is necessarily gifted for such a role.

- If you are seeking God on this:

  - Pray.

  - Evaluate yourself. What is your motivation? What are you hoping to accomplish for the kingdom by taking on a dual role?

- Discover and discern your gifts and talents. What specific gifts have you been given by God? What are you especially talented at?

- What experience do you already have that will enhance the effectiveness of your gifts and talents?

- What do you *enjoy* doing? God wants you to have life and have it abundantly. His will for your life should direct you down a path that is exciting and energizing for you.

- Wait upon the Lord. Don't rush a decision. If pursuing a dual role is from the Lord, he will make it clear to you, and he will bring people into your life who will affirm your call and provide doors of opportunity for you.

Whatever the specifics of our calling, our ultimate purpose is to give God the glory in all that we do. We can do this on the holy ground of his Church. And Jesus, if he chooses, can give us the privilege to do this on the holy ground of the business world.

Rising from the Rubble

How God Used Disaster to Raise Up
a New Leadership Generation

YOSHIYA HARI

"Pastor, we need your help." I was standing in the middle of a crowded office in Tokyo. All around me was chaos. Phones were ringing, televisions were blaring, and people were everywhere.

It was March 2011. A monstrous disaster had struck my country. A massive earthquake was soon followed by a lethal tsunami, resulting in the meltdown of one of our nuclear plants (known as the Triple Disaster). We would learn that tens of thousands of people had been killed and hundreds of thousands of people had been made homeless.

As soon as I was able, I had come to the headquarters of Christian Relief, Assistance, Support, and Hope Japan (CRASH), founded by foreign missionaries to provide assistance in a time of disaster. CRASH Japan was a small, young organization. It had been called upon to help only with smaller issues. Now, CRASH Japan was facing a disaster bigger than anyone had imagined possible.

"Pastor, we need you to head up our logistics effort. You will be in charge of coordinating the collection and distribution of relief supplies. Can you do it?" *Me? A young leader, not even forty years old? Do they know what they are asking?*

LIMITED LEADERS

JAPAN, MY NATIVE COUNTRY, has a strong heritage of leadership development. We are a group-centric culture, with life built around community. Over the centuries, we developed an apprenticeship system that created channels through which people could be trained and mentored for all manner of vocations—everything from plumbing to professional management.

We are also a culture that respects and reveres our elderly. The maturity that comes with age is highly valued—so much so that, in Japan, a person 50 years of age is still considered young in leadership terms. But while we are built around community, our system is hierarchical. Senior leaders have great authority and are given much respect. Senior leadership is not questioned, especially by younger leaders in the group. Japan has also had a culture of lifetime employment. When a person becomes a senior leader, they envision holding that position not to a particular retirement age, but until their death.

In addition to age, geography has created disparate perspectives on leadership. In Japan's major urban centers, cosmopolitan influence has loosened structures to some degree. But in our small towns and rural villages, things are more conservative. The limits placed on younger leaders in rural Japan are still quite rigid.

There are many strengths to our leadership structure. But it also creates barriers. Younger leaders who seek positions of greater responsibility and authority bump into rigid ceilings. It is expected that they will wait patiently, perhaps for many years, for their opportunity to become senior leaders. If that means waiting decades, so be it.

This commitment to a senior-centric, highly-defined hierarchy has created an inability to adjust to changing times and situations. In the 1970s and 80s, we were known as Japan, Inc. The rest of the world marveled at our economic model. We had built a system designed to make Japan a powerhouse for decades.

But when global economic circumstances changed, our system staggered. Suddenly, we no longer held the keys to long-term success. And worse, we could not seem to adapt our structures and approaches to regain our effectiveness. In many ways, the struggle continues to this day.

LIMITED LEADERS: CHURCH VERSION

THE SAME CULTURAL CONTEXT and structures that govern Japanese society in general exist in our churches. And we can add a biblical flavor to the context. I have heard of older pastors who will sit down with a younger leader frustrated by the lack of opportunity. "Remember I Peter 5:6," the older leader will say:

*Humble yourselves, therefore, under God's mighty
hand, that he may lift you up in due time.*

"Be patient. God will give you opportunity in his own good time."

After World War II, some of the first Japanese converts to Christianity–many of them in their 20s–became pastors and church leaders. They were strong personalities, forged out of the trials of the postwar era. Many of these leaders are still in charge to this day, even as they move into their 70s and 80s.

The next generation (now in their 50s and 60s) grew up in a time of economic growth and an easier life. They have been more passive, more comfortable with following rather than leading. My generation, however, was raised in a tougher era. Our economic bubble had burst, creating harder times. And there were more of us. Competition at school and in the workplace has been, and is, intense. The result is that we are more assertive, more inclined to want to assume responsibility and leadership. We feel the leadership ceiling more acutely than our predecessors.

As a pastor who began ministry in my 20s, I have experienced the process firsthand. And while I respect the strengths of our system, and honor the senior leaders under whom I have served, I am aware of the impact our system has on younger leaders like me...and the frustrations it can create.

But I am getting ahead of myself. Let me first share about the path God put me on that led to March 11, 2011–finding myself standing in the middle of a chaotic office, our country reeling from a major catastrophe, being asked to take charge of something I had never done before.

"THE EXPOSED NAIL SHOULD BE HAMMERED DOWN"

I WAS BORN INTO a Christian family. For my first five years, I thought the whole world was Christian. All I knew was my family, their Christian friends, and our little church. From my child's perspective, this was reality.

That perspective changed quickly when I started school. I became aware that as a Japanese Christian, I was part of a very small minority. One of my first vivid memories was our kindergarten graduation ceremony. "What do you want to be when you grow up?" We were asked. Each of us answered: "I want to be a pilot." "I want to be a doctor." "A firefighter." "A businessman." "A truck driver." Finally, it was my turn. "I want to become a pastor," I said. Silence enveloped the room as my classmates looked at me in wonder. "Wow," was all the parents could say.

But the reaction was not simply one of wonder. I quickly learned that the views and perspectives of my minority group were not well received. Before long, my friends began to tease me for my beliefs.

Japanese culture places a high value on conformity, on everyone thinking and acting alike. We have a saying in Japan: *The exposed nail should be hammered down.* As a Christian, I was an exposed nail. And my classmates were hammering away. The teasing turned to harassment and bullying. Life at school was becoming intolerable.

As a way to cope, I developed two faces–my Christian face and my school face. At home and church, I was a believer. But at school, I hid my Christian identity. I strove to fit in with my secular friends. It worked–so well, in fact, that I began to embrace my secular life.

The gap between my two identities widened in my junior high and high school years. At school, I became both a class leader and a life of the after-class parties. Life in church, however, was becoming miserable. I was stuck in what seemed to be a small, boring group. When I went to church at all, it was to sleep.

CROSSROADS TO A CALL

AT THE END OF 10TH GRADE, God got ahold of me at a Christian camp my parents made me attend. I met dozens of Christian boys and girls my age–young people with attractive character and strong faith. I was shocked, impressed, and convicted. Everything that was wrong about my double life came into focus. I realized I was at a crossroads. "God, I am ashamed," I prayed. "I have hidden myself because I was afraid to be an 'exposed nail.' I don't want to live like that anymore. I want to be known as a Christian–and I want to share the gospel with my friends." My life began to turn around, away from deceit and toward an embrace of my identity as a Christ follower.

I returned to school with a goal: before the year was finished, I would bring 10 friends to my church. Week after week, I would reach out to my friends: "Come to church with me. How about tomorrow?" By the end of the year, 13 friends had come to my church. And even more amazing in the Japanese context, one of my friends became a believer and was baptized.

I was learning more about myself. God seemed to have graced me with gifts for leadership. When I had been playing the two-faced game, these gifts brought me leadership positions at school. But when I rededicated my life to Christ, these gifts were used to draw my friends toward an encounter with our Lord. Either way, the gifts were there– to be used for temporal rewards or for eternal results.

This awareness was reinforced by my Sunday school teacher. We had just finished class and I was preparing to leave. As I turned to go, he shocked me with these words: "Maybe you should pray about becoming a pastor." I was reminded of my kindergarten dream. *Did God possibly want me to actually a pastor?*

God brought it all together on Easter Sunday. As the pastor preached out of John 21, God spoke to me through the story of Peter's encounter with Jesus. *Jesus called Peter, the man who denied him three times. Despite Peter's sin and failure, Jesus raised him up to lead his church. If Jesus could do that for Peter, perhaps he can do that for me.*

In a Baptist church like the one I attended, invitations are given. When the invitation was given that Easter, I raised my hand and went forward. "God has spoken to me this morning," I shared. "I believe that he is calling me into the ministry."

But there remained the matter of further education. As high school was ending, I took the university examinations. My scores did not qualify me for a top-level university, at least in the conventional sense. It turned out God had his own idea of a top-level university for me.

UNIVERSITY IN THE COUNTRYSIDE—AND PASTOR CHIDA

I WAS ACCEPTED TO Yamagata University, a school located in a distant, rural, and snowy part of the country. For someone born and raised in the Tokyo area, it was a transition. I knew it would be important for me to find a church home for my university years. That is where I met Pastor Chida.

To help explain the impact Pastor Chida had in my life, I must confess that, even with the harassment I experienced in my early years at school, I had had a pampered life. I was a favored boy growing up in my family and my church. I got a lot of strokes and affirmation at school. All in all, I had enjoyed a fairly easy life. It was with that background that I stepped up to Pastor Chida and told him, "I want to become a pastor." His reply was immediate: "Okay–then I will train you."

What could be hard to understand to someone unfamiliar with the Japanese context is how unusual Pastor Chida's response was. I have shared about the hierarchical structure that elevates and perpetuates senior leadership. One of the fallouts of this model is that there is little incentive for developing new leaders. "Leadership development" usually means years of servitude before becoming old enough to inherit one's own mantle of senior leadership. Active training and mentoring of younger, emerging leaders is deemphasized or simply ignored.

But this was not true of Pastor Chida. He was committed to raising up new leaders. And he was a drillmaster.

PASTORAL BOOT CAMP

MY PAMPERED LIFE and general immaturity came into a smashing collision with Pastor Chida's leader development model. He believed in rigorous training, begun immediately. His expectation was that I would launch at once into ministry–children's ministry, campus ministry, prayer meetings, revival meetings. All of this was expected of me while I maintained my full-time studies.

These expectations came without the strokes of affirmation I was accustomed to. Pastor Chida's style was that of a tough father. He was a man of few words and fewer compliments. You were expected to excel–praise was not part of the equation. On the other hand, criticism was part of the equation. Negative feedback was a regular part of the training.

At first, I thought Pastor Chida did not like me. But over time, I began to realize Pastor Chida expressed his love for me through his investment in my development as a leader.

In his view, true affirmation came through developing a leader empowered to shoulder responsibility, groomed through practical experience, tempered by trial and error, and equipped to then develop another leader. "A leader should produce one more leader" was his motto. And unlike the Japanese educational system, which stresses the acquisition of abstract knowledge, Pastor Chiba's boot camp emphasized not just knowledge, but the development of personal character.

In short, Pastor Chida was *coaching* me. In 1995, he had learned about coaching through Asian Access training. It had proven so fruitful compared to the traditional, top-down model of leader development that Pastor Chida immediately applied it to his ministry. By God's timing, I happened to come along just as Pastor Chida was transitioning to the coaching approach. Under his tutelage, I went from an arrogant boy to an experienced leader seeking to serve with humility. I was growing up.

LEFT TURN INTO THE MARKETPLACE

UPON GRADUATION, Pastor Chida recommended I go straight to seminary. But I felt a pull to return to my hometown. Many of my Christian friends back home were struggling in their faith. I wanted to go back, encourage them, and strengthen them with the discipleship principles I had learned under Pastor Chida.

Pastor Chida was not happy with my decision. But he decided to view it through the lens of ministry. Upon learning I had secured a job as an engineer in a printing company, his parting words to me were, "Go evangelize the workplace."

That turned out to be much more difficult than I had anticipated. Pastor Chida's expectations for my life were nothing compared to those of my new employers. We were expected to work long hours under extreme pressure. There was no time for any life outside of work. In addition, Japanese culture discourages discussing sensitive issues like religion with others for fear of disrupting group harmony. And as the youngest employee, I had no right to share anything with my older co-workers, especially something like the gospel. It was not long before I felt I had lost my way. *What am I doing here?* I asked myself. It seemed like I had hit a dead end.

One morning during my devotions, I felt like God was saying to me, "Take a day off from work and go do street ministry at the train station." I couldn't believe my ears–but I could not get the words out of my head. Finally, I decided to follow through. Obtaining permission for a day off, I headed to the Yokohama train station with a Bible and some gospel tracts.

No one wanted my tracts or wanted to talk to me. Finally, spiritually and emotionally exhausted, I sat on a bench. *Lord, I'm so powerless*, I prayed. *Please give me your power.* Looking up after my prayer, I saw an American man sitting to my left. For some reason, it occurred to me to try something I had never done before: Share the gospel with him–in English. So I did.

To my surprise, I discovered he was a Christian! He served as an English teacher at a church–the same kind of ministry that had reached my father so many years ago. We decided to get a cup of coffee and have a chat. As we talked, I began to pour out my struggles and my feeling of powerlessness. He startled me with a question: "What do you think about the Holy Spirit?" (I should mention at this point that I had grown up in a tradition that believed the gifts of the Spirit were no longer at work on the earth. In our world, Pentecostals were misguided believers.)

My friend shared his perspective on how the Holy Spirit was still at work in the world. "Jesus might be talking to you right now like he did to the disciples just before Pentecost," he told me:

> *On one occasion, while he was eating with them, he gave them this command: "Do not leave Jerusalem, but wait for the gift my Father promised, which you have heard me speak about. For John baptized with water, but in a few days you will be baptized with the Holy Spirit."*
>
> Acts 1:4-5

Before long, my new friend had to leave. "Can I pray for you before I go?" he asked. As he began to pray, I heard him begin to use another language. I realized he was doing what Pentecostals called "speaking in tongues," something totally foreign to my experience. It was astounding–but what was even more astounding was that, all at once, I began to do the same thing! Somehow, a new sort of language was coming out of me, in prayer. On that day, my personal book of Acts began.

My purpose here is not to begin a theological debate, but simply to share my journey. Despite my upbringing in a church that did not believe in the present-day manifestation of the gifts of the Spirit, I could not deny my experience. Inevitably, this led to my needing to move on from this denomination. But to where?

TURNING BACK TO THE MINISTRY

IT WAS TIME TO transition into what I knew to be my calling–the pastorate. But where could I actually serve? In good conscience, I could no longer serve in the denomination within which I grew up. What should I do? In my distress, I turned to someone I could trust: Pastor Chida.

Over dinner, I poured out my situation. "How can I fulfill the call God has placed on me to pastor when I can no longer serve in my denomination?" Pastor Chida had an idea: *Church-Based Theological Education* (CBTE). Along with a colleague who directed a separate seminary, Pastor Chida had set up a model where each student would spend three weeks at the school directed by Pastor Chida and one week at the school directed by his colleague. It was a combination of theological education and practical church experience blended into a simultaneous learning environment. CBTE was connected to Keisen ("Grace Spring") Christ Church, a network of 14 venues of which Pastor Chida's church is a part.

CBTE turned out to be the answer for me. I moved back to Yamagata and began a three-year course of study. Along the way I met Megumi, a fellow student who had felt called to resign her teaching job to enter seminary. She is now my wife.

INTO THE FIRE: FIRST PASTORATE

IN 2003, I BECAME pastor of Saikyo Hope Chapel. SHC had been founded in the 1990s by an American missionary. After some fruitful years, the church ran into difficulties. The missionary felt the need to move out of the situation and advocated for Japanese leadership to be brought in. With that, we received the call. I was 29 years old.

At that time, SHC was in a precarious position. There were perhaps 20 members, most of them occasional attenders. I got a sense of the level of commitment when, on the Sunday of my ordination, all but a few of the congregants left the building immediately after church ended, before the ordination service was to begin. Within a month, I realized the core group of my church consisted of two faithful saints, both in their 70s. We were starting from scratch.

A MOST UNLIKELY CATALYST

THE MOST UNUSUAL member of our little congregation was an awkward young man with tattered clothes and a strange haircut. Ishida wasn't just quiet—he did not speak. His look and demeanor shouted *rebel*. It was hard to understand why he was at church in the first place.

Then one Sunday, he came up to me and actually spoke. "Pastor, I am going to distribute food and share the gospel with the homeless people under the local bridge. Would you come with me?"

A whole new world, and a whole new understanding of my mysterious congregant, opened up as Ishida took me to his regular place of ministry. Having grown up a poorly performing student with no friends, Ishida had lived a virtually homeless life for many years. Having somewhat stabilized his life, he had developed a burden for the homeless. "I was like them," he told me. "They need the touch of Jesus, just like I did. I would like to start a homeless church."

Ishida became my first ministry trainee. We began to meet every week for Bible study. For all of his eccentricities, I came to realize that Ishida was faithful. When he saw a command from God, he obeyed. When I gave him instruction, he responded. Despite his awkwardness, Ishida reached many people for Christ. He combined evangelistic gifts with a soft heart.

Ishida became a catalyst for our church. "People need Jesus," he would say. "We can reach them." The example of his life was both inspiring and challenging. Members of the church could see that he backed up his words with his actions. Little by little, people in our church began to catch a vision for how they might reach their neighbors.

A few years into our study, Ishida decided to quit his job. The printing company he worked for printed pornographic magazines, which he did not want to support. "What will you do for work?" I asked him. "The Lord will provide," he answered.

The very next day, a Christian businessman showed up, unannounced, at the church–a highly unusual occurrence. "We want to start a welfare center for the elderly," this businessman told me. "We are looking for qualified staff. Do you know any good people?" Shortly thereafter, Ishida was hired, and eventually worked his way up to manager.

Eight years after we began our Bible study, Ishida entered seminary. Three years later, he was ordained and commissioned as a full-time evangelist. He is now a senior pastor in northern Japan. My trainee is a leader in his own right.

GROWING CHURCH, EXPANDING ROLES

OVER THE YEARS, our church began to grow. God began to expand my vision for the world and ministry through short-term mission trips to India. And by 2010, I began to get personally restless. The pastorate, for all of its blessings, left me feeling cut off from the real world. I felt a pull to return to a setting like my old printing job where I would regularly rub shoulders with nonbelievers. And Ichida's commissioning as an evangelist increased the financial burden for the church. *Maybe I'll get a regular job again*, I thought. *It will reconnect me with society and I can help to finance Ichida's ministry.*

As I was pondering all this, I got a surprising call. The *Japan Church Growth Institute* (now known as Asian Access Japan) had been training pastors in Japan for more than 40 years. I myself had participated in a JCGI class in 2008-2009. Their director was transitioning and JCGI was looking for new leadership. Would I be open to applying for the position of director? While part time, it was a type of position usually reserved for a leader much senior to me.

The call left me overwhelmed. *I'm not worthy*, I thought. *I'm too young, too inexperienced. They have an artificially high view of me.* It seemed out of the question that I should be a candidate.

It was at that time that I again visited India. While there, I heard about a number of Hindu converts to Christianity who had returned back to their Hindu roots. What happened, I asked? "We do not have enough qualified leaders to adequately disciple and shepherd new converts," I was told. "Too many new believers slip through the cracks and disappear back into Hinduism."

The crying need for leader training was right before my eyes. What about my country? Was God calling me to help to develop leaders in Japan? Pastor Chida's words came back to me: "A leader should produce one more leader." In 2010, I was commissioned as director of JCGI, to begin in 2011.

PROTECTING THE EXPOSED NAIL

IF MY STORY SOUNDS highly unusual for a younger leader in Japan, it is because it is. And I deeply apologize for what must seem like boasting. But my unusual rise as a younger leader only serves to highlight the barriers my peers face in Japan.

As I mentioned earlier, the leadership structures in Japan are hierarchical, favor seniority, and are inflexible. For most younger leaders, these structures are immovable. There are solid ceilings that limit what emerging leaders are able to do. And in Japanese society, it would be highly impolite for those emerging leaders to protest about their situation.

Even for someone in my privileged position, the limits were there. I might be commissioned director of JCGI, but would older leaders acknowledge my leadership? Would they respect me? Or would I be a director in name only?

This was the environment when our world was turned upside down—March 11, 2011.

LEADERSHIP NEEDED—NOW

THE FIRST DAYS AFTER the disaster were chaotic. Our government agencies were there, doing all that they could. But the scope of the disaster was so vast that everyone's help was needed.

Into this breach stepped the Church in Japan. From all over the country, believers collected supplies and raised money. Many brought these resources directly to the disaster sites. Thousands of Christians looked for ways they could volunteer. Everyone wanted to help. What was desperately needed were leaders. Leaders were needed who could get on site, assess the situation, and coordinate the efforts to provide immediate help and ongoing care.

As I tried to get a grasp on my new duties at CRASH Japan, this passage from Matthew 9:35-38 became my heart prayer:

> *Jesus went through all the towns and villages, teaching in their synagogues, proclaiming the good news of the kingdom and healing every disease and sickness. When he saw the crowds, he had compassion on them, because they were harassed and helpless, like sheep without a shepherd. Then he said to his disciples, "The harvest is plentiful but the workers are few. Ask the Lord of the harvest, therefore, to send out workers into his harvest field."*

This prayer was being echoed by a friend of mine. He lived in Tohoku, in the middle of the disaster area. Like me, he was a younger leader, accustomed to limited leadership under the authority of older, more senior leaders. "Lord, send workers," he prayed. He saw himself as one of those workers, preparing to serve under older authority as soon as senior leadership arrived on site.

But he *became* one of the senior leaders. The disaster area was so chaotic that the need for leaders was immediate. Those on site, like my friend, had to step up. Additionally, the sheer physical stress of the disaster sites made it difficult, if not impossible, for senior leaders in their 60s, 70s, and 80s to function there effectively for any period of time.

Younger leaders, on the other hand, had the physical stamina and energy to handle the stresses of the disaster-area environments. They could commit time to the work as they were not burdened with as many ongoing responsibilities as their senior leaders. The circumstances of the Triple Disaster had created a vacuum–space where these emerging leaders had room to step up and lead in a situation that desperately needed their leadership.

It was nothing that anyone would ever plan for. And I do not know why natural disasters happen. But in his mercy, God can use even something as awful as the Triple Disaster for good. In our case, God used the crying needs created by the catastrophe to raise up a generation of emerging leaders far more quickly, being given far more authority and responsibility, than ever would have happened under normal circumstances.

Life for my country had changed forever. And although we didn't realize it at the time, life for leaders in the Japanese Church was also beginning to change.

SEISMIC LEADERSHIP CHANGE

AS YOUNGER PASTORS and Christian leaders continued to serve in the relief, rebuilding, and ongoing ministry efforts, a seismic shift began within the leadership structures of the Church in Japan. Emerging leaders were gaining hands-on experience. More and more, they were being asked to take on lead roles. And they were increasingly being viewed as senior leaders in their own right.

At the same time, the self-image of these leaders was also changing. They began to grow into their expanded roles. Their confidence in their leadership abilities also grew. They began to see themselves as leaders capable of shouldering the senior-level responsibilities being thrust upon them. They began to consider that a new paradigm for leadership in the Japanese Church might be possible.

As the years went by, the effects of the disaster began to ebb. In the communities where rebuilding was possible, homes were rebuilt and people began to return. While things will never be back to what they were before the Triple Disaster, life began to return to something resembling normal. But the leadership environment for the Church in Japan was never going back to "normal."

SENIOR LEADERS: THE CHALLENGE OF RE-ENTRY

AS THINGS SLOWLY returned to something like normal life, many leaders resumed the positions they had held before the disaster. But things had changed. Senior leaders now related to younger colleagues who possessed a new confidence and sense of value. These younger leaders were ready to continue to expand their roles and responsibilities. Senior leaders were undergoing a re-entry experience. They resumed their old positions of authority...but in an environment where the standards, norms, and expectations had all changed.

It has been an unsettling experience. Some senior leaders have adapted well to the new environment. For others, the adjustment has proven to be challenging. It is an ongoing process that continues to this day, and will continue into the future. But it is continuing. There is no way to rewind to what life was like before the disaster. God is taking us into a new season.

We recently experienced this phenomenon again. In April 2016, two earthquakes struck Kumamoto in Southern Japan. At least 49 people were killed and 3,000 injured. Extensive damage was done to the area. People were needed immediately to lead the relief and rebuilding efforts.

The Church's response is being coordinated by a friend of mine. Like me, he is a pastor in his 40s. Once again, a disaster has placed a younger leader in a senior position.

THE NEW REALITY—BENEFITS, CHALLENGES

PETER CHAO, FOUNDER of Eagles Communications in Singapore, speaks of the Estuary Effect. "In an estuary, salt water and fresh water mingle together. The result of this mingling is a vibrant ecosystem. In the same way, when people in leadership can mingle across hierarchical and structural lines, it can spark vibrant growth in the organization's ecosystem."

This Estuary Effect has been one of the benefits that the circumstances of the disaster have brought to our leadership structure in the Church in Japan. By necessity, older and younger leaders have mingled. Roles and responsibilities have interchanged. Levels of authority have evolved and varied as circumstances have altered. The barriers that separated senior and younger leaders here have been shaken. The result has been vibrant growth.

It's possible that this shaking up of the old barriers–this Spirit-driven Estuary Effect–could help us address the greatest challenge facing the cause of Christ in Japan: the chronic spiritual poverty of our country.

It is vexing to me that Japan–a wealthy, developed country–is known in the Christian mission world as a *spiritually poor country*. The facts cannot be ignored. After decades of intense, dedicated, prayer-driven efforts by Japanese Christians and foreign missionaries, the Christian population in my country still runs below two percent. Our evangelistic work has not resulted in a meaningful increase in the number of people coming to Christ. The Church in Japan at this time is losing more members through death than it is replacing. At this rate, we run the risk of shrinking to almost nothing.

Japanese and foreign believers alike have wracked their brains and their hearts, attempting to understand why my country is such a difficult mission field. There are likely many factors–but could one of them be the rigidity built into our understanding of leadership and leadership development? Just as our government and business leaders, who share the same inflexible system, have been unable to adjust from the economic setbacks of the 1990s, are we Japanese Christians unable to adjust to meet the authentic spiritual needs of our fellow Japanese because of our own inflexibility?

But...is it possible that the Estuary Effect created by our response to the disaster could be the beginning of a new season of ministry: a time when the Church in Japan authentically connects with our people, and when ministry is led by a combination of gifted leaders, younger as well as older, working together in mutual respect and collaboration? If this happens, then God in his wisdom has brought forth good, even from a disaster as horrible as the earthquake, tsunami, and nuclear meltdown of 2011.

We are very early in the journey. There is still much to do, and many barriers to overcome. But it could be that a new generation of God's leaders are emerging, empowered for ministry and mission in ways not before seen in my country...rising out of the rubble.

No Separation

An Asian Woman's Journey into Pastoral Leadership

ALMA KYAW THURA

"Mrs. Kyaw Thura, we are sorry. But you are going to have to make a decision. You will either have to bring New Life in Christ ministries under the authority of the church, or you will have to find somewhere else to conduct your ministry.

"Remember, we pay your husband's salary. You answer to us."

Sadness and anger ran through me as I listened to these words. I was sitting in the parsonage that my husband Wesley and I shared at Yangon Methodist English Church, where he had been pastor for 12 years. Surrounding me was a group of church leaders and elders. They had come to inform me that the ministry God had given me was no longer welcome at the church.

What should my husband and I decide? If I insisted on continuing the ministry at the church, it could mean Wesley's dismissal as pastor. But if I agreed to their terms, I would lose any authority I had been given by God to reach out to poor and marginalized Buddhists with the love of

Jesus Christ. And I would be bowing to the authority of "leaders" who, despite their church titles, had no viable ministry or witness.

As Wesley and I listened and prayed, I reflected on the journey that had led us to this confrontation. It was a long, twisting path that God had placed me on in my childhood. And it led not only to this tense meeting, but to a new awareness of God's call on my life as a wife, mother...and minister of the gospel.

TURBULENT UPBRINGING, GLIMMERS OF FAITH

THE OLDEST OF THREE children, I was born into a dynamic, interfaith household. My father, a high-level government official, was Buddhist. He converted to Christ when he was 45 years old, living as a Christ follower until his death at 70. My mother, who is still with us, was a believer who grew up in a Christian family. She was also an accomplished track and field athlete, winning three gold medals in the Asia Games.

When I was a baby, my father was arrested and imprisoned for five years on a corruption charge. The offense had been committed by an officer under his authority, but because it had happened under his watch, my father took the blame for his junior officer's crime.

With my father in prison and my mother away pursuing her athletic career, I was brought up by my grandmother. She had a strong Christian faith and a pure British culture. She trained me to be Western in my thinking and behavior, which is much different from the traditional Burmese style. I gained a natural self-discipline and set of manners that do not usually exist in Burmese culture.

When I was four years old, a life-threatening crisis served as a kind of prophecy for what was to come in my adult years. Our family had taken in and housed a homeless woman. To our peril, she turned out to be a predator. She put ground glass into our rice and poison into our water. One day, this woman threw an iron shot-put at me and hit me in the eyebrow. I was hospitalized in critical condition, but God healed me. We eventually discovered–when she was arrested and put in jail for murder–that the woman had killed a man and run to Yangon, where she found refuge with us.

UNIVERSITY ENROLLMENT, SPIRITUAL TRANSFORMATION

BY THE TIME I reached tenth standard (the completion of high school at that time), I was a Christian, but in name only. My faith meant little to my life. My focus was to get out of my country, get to the United States, get rich, and stay in the United States forever. I had no interest in the poor and needy in my country. Reaching out to them with the love of Christ never occurred to me.

My plans were thwarted when the United States rejected my visa application. I was angry with God: "You know that I want to leave here. Why don't you let me go to the United States?" At that time, I had no understanding of God's plan for my life in my home country.

I entered university and began my higher education. Wesley and I had met by then and saw each other often. That first year, a pastor friend of Wesley's visited us. In a conversation, he asked me a question: "Alma, if you died tonight, where would your spirit go?" I realized that I did not really know the answer. His question made me fearful of death. But then this pastor followed up his question by sharing the salvation message of the gospel with me. I came to understand the grace of Jesus and the opportunity I had to repent of my sins and accept Jesus Christ as my Lord and Savior. This I did.

NEW LIFE, NEW BURDEN

IMMEDIATELY UPON MY receiving Christ, God gave me a burden for the poor and needy in our country. Many of the poor in Myanmar are day laborers and menial workers, barely scratching out a living. Many are hard-core Buddhists, especially in their culture. They are considered almost impossible to reach. But I wanted to reach out to them with the saving love of Jesus.

This burden became an actual pain in my heart. I so wanted to share the gospel, but I did not know how. I prayed that God would teach me how to share his good news. God answered my prayers. He showed me that the best way to begin a saving relationship with those for whom I had such a burden was to first share my life testimony, then seek to help them practically as much as I could. God began to give me the courage to follow through.

But even as I sought to get out and share the gospel, I experienced a setback. I was afflicted with heart and breathing problems, and I was hospitalized four times. My physical afflictions imposed significant limitations on my ability to come alongside others and share my life and God's truth with them. One avenue of blessing did emerge from this time of illness and limitation: God inspired me to focus more on prayer ministry, an outreach I was able to do no matter what my physical condition.

TRANSITION TO A TRADITIONAL LIFE

WESLEY AND I WERE married in 1998. God blessed us with two children, our son Trust and our daughter Phoebe. Wesley began his ministry career as a church pastor and I began a traditional life as a wife and mother.

In those early years, we faced many challenges. Wesley's salary was quite small and we struggled financially. Raising a family of four on a pastor's income required thrift and ingenuity. As Wesley's wife, I embraced the traditional female roles of wife and mother. I stayed in the background and focused on the business of running our household.

The burden that God had given me to reach others for Christ, especially the poor and needy in our community, was still there. I took every chance to share the gospel with people who visited our home. But it seemed that to fulfill the responsibilities of my traditional life, I would have to set aside my burden, vision, and mission.

I did attempt to see God's vision made real through our Methodist Women's Fellowship. As a pastor's wife, I was naturally a part of this group. And over time, I became president of the fellowship. But MWF was, for its members, primarily a social network. The idea of collaborating for ministry was not a priority.

When I became president, I tried to get our members involved in evangelism, discipleship, and outreach to the poor and needy around us. This was not well received. Eventually, pressure from influential women in the group resulted in my being removed from my leadership post. It seemed I would not be able to fulfill God's call for my life after all.

MY WORLD UPTURNED: LIFE-THREATENING DIAGNOSIS

FOR WHATEVER REASONS, God had placed significant physical challenges in my life over the years. As a little girl, I had nearly been killed by that iron shot-put. As a university student, I was afflicted with significant heart and breathing problems. But in 2004, I received the biggest blow of all.

The doctors diagnosed me with late-stage ovarian cancer. They began a brutal six-round chemotherapy regimen, even while they told me I probably had about six months to live. The chemotherapy was devastating. After two rounds, I had become a virtual skeleton and could barely function. It was a living death, with only the "hope" of keeping me alive for a few more months.

A NEW VISION

ONE DAY, I was resting at home after my second round of chemotherapy. Suddenly, I heard a call: "Alma, Alma." When I looked around, I saw a very tall man, dressed in white. He was like an angel. He then said, "There are seven boxes on your pillow. They are not your own. They are Almighty God's Treasure." With that, he disappeared.

Immediately I saw a vision. In the vision, I was opening up my pillow and found a small box. When I opened the box, I found ordinary stones–but then a second box came out of the first box, bigger than the first! Again, there were ordinary stones inside this box–but once again, a third box came out of this second box. Inside this box, there were precious stones–and a fourth box, then a fifth, each also containing precious stones. Then a sixth box came out, much bigger than all the rest...and this box was filled with the finest gold! I waited, expecting a seventh box. But the sixth box was the last–no seventh box ever appeared.

When Wesley arrived home, I shared the vision with him. He suggested we pray together in hopes of understanding or interpreting the vision. We prayed along these lines for some time. Finally, God gave us the meaning of his vision:

- The boxes meant *process*
- The ordinary stones meant *beginning stages of new believers*
- The bigger boxes coming out of smaller boxes meant *growing step by step*

- The precious stones meant *as new believers are being nurtured, they become precious and qualified to be built as the Holy House of God*

- The gold meant *they become mature believers and good examples for others*

- The mysterious seventh box that never appeared meant *the rest is of God*

God then reinforced what he had shared in the vision through some key Scriptures:

As you come to him, the living Stone—rejected by humans but chosen by God and precious to him—you also, like living stones, are being built into a spiritual house to be a holy priesthood, offering spiritual sacrifices acceptable to God through Jesus Christ.

1 Peter 2:4-5

The LORD's right hand is lifted high;
the LORD's right hand has done mighty things!
I will not die but live,
and will proclaim what the LORD has done.

Psalm 118:16-17

Jesus looked at them and said,
"With man this is impossible, but with God all things are possible."

Matthew 19:26

Then Jesus said, "Did I not tell you that if you believe, you will
see the glory of God?"

John 11:40

The vision God had given me, reinforced by his Word, led me to believe that God would indeed heal me of my cancer. I decided to stop the chemotherapy after the second round and trust God for my life.

STOP THE TREATMENT, START THE HEALING

UPON HEARING OF MY decision to stop treatment, some people were quite critical. Others thought I had gone crazy. But many of my friends stood firm with me and trusted that God's power would be manifest in my life.

My doctor was quite worried, but she respected my decision. "Come in every six months for tests," she told me. (She was courteous enough not to add, "If you are still alive.") I agreed to begin this regular regimen. For the next three years, I went in regularly, every six months, and was tested. My doctor was astounded. "The tests show that you are now cancer free," she told me. God had healed me!

Our God is a healing God. In my case, the Lord not only cured me of ovarian cancer–he freed me from three illnesses that had plagued me for decades: ischemic heart disease, chronic sinus/breathing problems, and swelling of the stomach. At this time, I am blessed with complete health.

My response to God's miraculous healing was, "Tell everybody!" I wanted to serve God with a fresh sense of gratitude for his goodness and a fresh energy to pursue his calling on my life. I could not stop myself from sharing my testimony with everyone I met, at every opportunity.

And over time, an interesting thing happened: the more I shared, the more powerful my testimony seemed to become. People began to respond. I realized that more and more people were coming to Christ through hearing of Jesus' touch in my life. And many of these people were Buddhists from the laborer classes—those who are considered almost impossible to reach. God was using the fruit of his work in my life to bear greater fruit.

SECOND TRANSFORMATION:
NEW LIFE IN CHRIST MINISTRIES

GOD'S HEALING, AND the vision he gave me during my treatment, led me back to the original burden, vision, and mission that God had given me back in university. I rededicated my life to this original calling—to reach out to the poor, the marginalized, the low-status people, those considered the hardest to reach for Christ in my country.

In accepting this calling, I felt that God was directing me to serve as a fully empowered pastor, equipped to teach, preach, baptize, and serve communion. Essentially, I felt that God was calling and equipping me to perform any ministry function that a male pastor can do.

This is a radical concept in my country. Male hierarchy is still the predominant model for our society, and for leadership in ministry. But God provided me scriptural confirmation of the legitimacy of this call:

"'In the last days, God says,
I will pour out my Spirit on all people.
Your sons and daughters will prophesy,
your young men will see visions,
your old men will dream dreams.
Even on my servants, both men and women,
I will pour out my Spirit in those days,
and they will prophesy."

Acts 2:17-18

Then they called them in again and commanded them
not to speak or teach at all in the name of Jesus. But Peter
and John replied, "Which is right in God's eyes: to listen
to you, or to him? You be the judges! As for us, we cannot
help speaking about what we have seen and heard."

Acts 4:18-20

"Therefore go and make disciples of all nations, baptizing them
in the name of the Father and of the Son and of the Holy Spirit,

*and teaching them to obey everything I have commanded you.
And surely I am with you always, to the very end of the age."*

Matthew 28:19-20

My walk with God has always been a walk of obedience, one step at a time. I did not know what the future would hold, but I realized it was time for the next step of obedience. In September 2008, in our apartment, New Life in Christ ministries began.

A HUMBLE BEGINNING

ONE DAY, I LOOKED outside of my window and saw a woman walking slowly in the scorching sun. She was clearly a street vendor, a low-income, low-status position in my country. As I watched her, something in my heart told me to invite her into my home and offer her my hospitality. Such an invitation from a higher-status person to a lower-status person is very unusual in my country. The woman was quite puzzled and even a little nervous about my invitation, but she came in.

After providing her with some much needed food and drink, I listened to her as she shared her story of hardship. I was able to share some of my story and about the unconditional love of Jesus. Reinforced by the tangible hospitality I had been able to offer her in addition to my words, the woman was open to hearing about the gospel. We parted with the promise that my husband and I would try to visit her at her home and continue to develop our relationship.

About three weeks later, my husband and I were able to visit this woman in her slum community. Knowing that this was a poor community, we brought food and some simple supplies as a gesture of friendship and an expression of the love of Christ.

My new friend introduced us to her family and neighbors as she shared the story of our first encounter. God gave me the opportunity to share my healing testimony and the gospel of Christ. The response was startling. Immediately, several people responded "Yes" to accepting Christ as their Savior! This kind of soul-winning experience is highly unusual in my country and culture. But God was moving, and moving quickly. Our new friends–impoverished day laborers usually shunned by higher levels of society–were eager to know more about a God who loved them and wanted to do a healing work in their lives.

THE MINISTRY GROWS—AND SO DO THE PROBLEMS

IT BECAME CLEAR that these new believers needed to be discipled as soon as possible. They were beginning their journey as Christ followers from scratch, with no previous background or knowledge of the Bible, the Christian faith, or living the Christian life. In addition, these low-status day laborers were starting from a very disadvantaged position in life, a hard life that often leads to moral and physical decay. There was much to do.

We began by opening our home each Wednesday for an informal discipleship group. There, we tackled the multitude of spiritual, physical, moral, and life-management problems faced by our new brothers and sisters in Christ. The group grew quickly; quite soon, it became apparent that we needed a bigger place in which to meet.

As I mentioned at the beginning of this chapter, my husband at this time was serving as pastor of Yangon Methodist English Church, the leading Methodist church in the city. (You can read my husband's full story in "Losing My Face to Find My Soul: An Asian Pastor's Journey from Career to Calling," p. 7.) I went to the church leaders and requested that we be able to use the church sanctuary each Saturday for our discipleship meetings. They agreed, and our group quickly grew to over 100 adults and 30+ children, meeting each Saturday for evangelism, spiritual equipping, and life development. Each Saturday was a dynamic, even chaotic, adventure as our upper-class church members began to rub shoulders with my uneducated, unrefined day laborers.

It was not long before misunderstandings, jealousies, and class prejudices began to infect the situation. I began to get pressure from some key leaders to find another place to meet, off of the Methodist church compound. I began to push back. And while I felt God had given me an authentic call to lead this ministry, I was young in experience. I needed to develop my leadership skills in an increasingly stormy situation.

THE ASIAN ACCESS LEARNING OPPORTUNITY

JUST AS THE SITUATION was growing increasingly tense, God provided me the opportunity to join the fourth class of Asian Access Myanmar (also known as A2). In addition to his pastoral duties, my husband Wesley had been part of Asian Access Myanmar from its beginnings in 2003. His life had been powerfully transformed by his participation in the first class. I realized that I could greatly benefit from participating in an A2 learning community. I jumped at the chance to become a participant.

Over two and a half years, God used A2 to build into my life. My love relationship with God deepened. I gained insight on how to strengthen my marriage and family life as well as my ministry. Sessions led by pastors such as Eddy Leo, Abe Huber, and Bob Moffitt equipped me to reach souls, make disciples, develop leaders, and plant multiplying churches. More than anything, A2 helped me to discern the difference between spiritual authority and positional authority. God used my A2 training to confirm the legitimacy of my calling, as a woman and as a leader. And A2 helped me to understand that my love relationship with God is the foundation for my family, ministry, and leadership life.

THE TURBULENT ROAD TO FREEDOM IN CHRIST

UNFORTUNATELY, OPPOSITION to both the New Life in Christ ministry and my functioning as a fully empowered pastor and leader continued to grow. Resistance to the presence of poor, low-status Buddhists "polluting" our prestigious church campus increased. The standoff was reaching the point of no return.

Despite the pressure, by God's grace I remained true to my calling. I knew that I had to remain faithful to the call that God had put on my life. Throughout this time, my husband Wesley was an amazing support. He stood by me as his ministry career was placed in jeopardy. Together, we decided that we were willing to face the consequences of obeying God, no matter what happened.

The consequences were not long in coming. Wesley was removed from his position as lead pastor and transferred to a low-paying, junior staff position at one of our denomination's most hopeless congregations. We were evicted from our parsonage home and left to fend for our own housing–which we found impossible to afford on the lower salary. It was a deliberate demotion and humiliation. In our culture, this intentional stripping of one's face is meant to be devastating.

It was time for us to decide. Did we really trust God for our finances, our food, and our shelter? Did we really believe that he would look after us and our children if we were willing to step completely out on faith? We struggled with fear and anxiety...but we trusted as best we could that God would be faithful to his promises. We stepped out, left our old life behind, and launched the first New Life in Christ church.

THE LAND AND BUILDING MIRACLE

WE HAD STEPPED OUT—but where would we go? What would we do? How would we start?

God immediately made his presence known. We were presented with a miraculous gift of land in the north part of the city, graciously offered by friends and supporters who believed in our vision. By faith, we began to build a combination church and home upon this land, as God made the resources available.

Every day was another step of faith. Every day we again saw God at work. Yes, we still struggled with fear and anxiety. We are human. But even in our weakness, God honored our small steps of faith with amazing demonstrations of his power and goodness.

Within nine months, our church and home was built. The mother church for New Life in Christ ministries was a reality.

PRESENT DAY: CALLED TO LEAD

AT THE TIME OF THIS writing, our New Life in Christ ministries continue to be blessed by God. In our home congregation, 150 people now meet regularly. Our flock continues to be working-poor, low-status Buddhists. Daily, more and more of them—considered to be virtually unreachable—leave Buddhism behind and embrace Christ.

Our ministry continues to focus on meeting practical needs along with spiritual needs. We are regularly involved in the distribution of food and medicine. We offer vocational training in skills like sewing and flower arrangement. We are developing and managing microfinance networks. And we are raising tuition money to enable children to attend school.

Our approach to discipleship includes practical life counseling. Currently, eight cell groups are functioning. Our vision is to divide them into multiplying microcells in the near future. Phone ministry provides daily spiritual equipping. In these daily calls, we listen to people's problems, provide practical and spiritual counsel, and guide them in their daily walk with God.

We now provide shelter and daily provisions for two elderly couples who have become Christ followers and joined our fellowship. We continue to share Christ with them and build into their lives through a weekly time of discipleship.

Many children have come into our ministry who are from difficult backgrounds. Some have parents who are in prison on drug-related charges; some are from broken homes; and we have some precious ones whose parents have died. In the near future, we plan to provide shelter, food, and access to education for these vulnerable children.

We are beginning to see fruit from our efforts. Families are beginning to be able to stand on their own feet. Some families are even beginning to support the church through their tithes, offerings, and volunteer labor.

Evangelism remains at the heart of our ministry. Twice a month, church members share their testimonies and the gospel message to the many seekers attending our church and cell groups. Men, women, and children are being added into the kingdom of God every day.

A DAILY EXERCISE OF FAITH

SO HOW DO WE LIVE? By faith, one day at a time. We trust God for even our daily bread. And he provides.

In our Asian Access program, Rev. Jim Millard taught on "How to Know God's Will for Your Life." One of the key concepts he taught was, "Confirm God's guidance through multiple factors." In other words, seek confirmation from God that you are indeed aligned with his will from a number of different sources.

One major source that God has used to confirm our decision is through his provision. Each day, each week, each month, resources have come forth. We have been able to feed our family, maintain a home, keep our children in school, and oversee the development and growth of the ministry–all through the faithfulness of God and the generosity of his people.

I won't say there aren't stressful times. We can struggle to believe during the times that we watch our earthly resources dwindle down. We cry out to God as we seek to hear his voice. But over and over again, God proves himself faithful. We are here, we are alive, and we are blessed.

God has used our steps of faith to strengthen my spiritual walk. Because we must trust him for our daily bread, hearing God's voice has become part of my daily spiritual walk. I am motivated to keep my love relationship with God my first priority, every day.

VISION FOR THE FUTURE

GOD IS GIVING US an exciting vision for the future of New Life in Christ ministries. We are believing God to plant a second NLIC congregation about 25 kilometers (15 miles) from Yangon. We are investing deeply in the development of our people, most of whom are new believers in Christ. Our vision is:

- Everyone a disciple
- Spiritual, social, and life-circumstances growth
- Everyone growing in wisdom and maturity
- The fruitful path: from servant leaders to church planters to church multipliers

And God is raising up powerful grassroots leaders from our current church. These are not educated or trained ministers in the classic sense. They come from the bottom—the hardcore working poor of Yangon. But they are faithful disciples who are growing into leadership.

REFLECTIONS: RESPECT THE CULTURE, OBEY THE CALL

AS I REFLECT ON where God has brought me, thank you for allowing me an opportunity to share some perspectives as an Asian, a woman, and a Christian leader.

My understanding of our identity as Christ followers is grounded in *the priesthood of all believers*. There is no separation between the roles of a woman pastor and a male pastor. Like my male colleagues, I must be ready to do what God has called me to do. And God has called me, reinforcing his call through key Scriptures that have spoken into my life.

But while I am fully comfortable with my call as a woman leader, I believe that serving in the Asian context does require me to combine courage with sensitivity. To be effective, I must embrace the values expressed in Scripture passages like these:

"Behold, I am sending you out as sheep in the midst of wolves, so be wise as serpents and innocent as doves."

Matthew 10:16 (ESV)

"I have the right to do anything," you say–but not everything is beneficial. "I have the right to do anything"–but not everything is constructive.

1 Corinthians 10:23

Asian contexts and customs often prescribe specific roles for men and women. And the Christian community is as conservative about these roles as the rest of our society, if not more. For example, when people arrive at someone's home, there are cultural rules for where everyone should sit, prescribed by gender. To respect this protocol is polite, while to ignore it is rude. Also, when a group of women would call upon a home, it is considered appropriate to converse about everyday matters. But if these women would begin to share about spiritual matters, the man of the house would get up and leave. In our culture, discussion of religious matters is something a man should lead.

As a woman leader, I strive to honor and respect our culture as much as possible. So when I enter a home, I will sit in my prescribed place as a woman. But I will not allow our culture to suppress the call God has given me to serve as a pastor and as a leader. At that point, God's call overrides the cultural expectations. So if I am given an opportunity to share the gospel, I will take that opportunity.

Navigating the cultural minefields is challenging. The decisions are many, and complicated. But it is part of my call as a woman called to be a minister of the gospel of Christ. And I believe it is part of the call God places on any woman he empowers to serve as a leader for the sake of the kingdom.

SOME FINAL WORDS OF ENCOURAGEMENT FOR MY SISTER LEADERS

MORE AND MORE, women are becoming active in the working world, in public life, and in the church. Unfortunately, many limitations still exist for women, including in the church.

When we do not let women serve, work, speak, and yes, lead, we weaken ourselves. This is especially true for followers of Jesus. When we hold women down in ways that God never intended, we weaken the cause of Christ. We cripple the kingdom of God.

The good news is, when *all* Christ followers are empowered—women as well as men—to fulfill their God-given calls, we unleash a powerful force for good. The true oneness of the body of Christ is manifest. The world benefits. And the kingdom wins.

> *He told them, "The harvest is plentiful, but the workers are few. Ask the Lord of the harvest, therefore, to send out workers into his harvest field."*

Luke 10:2

So in Christ Jesus you are all children of God through faith, for all of you who were baptized into Christ have clothed yourselves with Christ. There is neither Jew nor Gentile, neither slave nor free, nor is there male and female, for you are all one in Christ Jesus. If you belong to Christ, then you are Abraham's seed, and heirs according to the promise.

Galatians 3:26-29

What encouragement can I offer my sisters in Christ who have been called to leadership? I believe God has gifted us with qualities that will enable us to persevere no matter what challenges lie before us. We are graced with patience. We are often experienced with long-suffering. We can have a mothering spirit. These qualities can give us the strength to withstand and overcome the cultural barriers and emotional minefields we will inevitably encounter.

The key to not only surviving, but thriving, is staying true to God's proven path:

- Keep your love relationship with God your #1 priority

- Seek the will of God

- Listen for his voice

- Obey what you hear

As you obey him, your obedience will give birth to a spirit of courage. God will then confirm his call for you through a multitude of sources. And ultimately, God will bring forth fruit from your efforts.

We have only one life with which to serve the Lord. Our call is precious. So obey him!

Sharing Credit
In a Guru-Centered World

Counter-Cultural Leadership in an Asian Context

LEOR SARKAR

"You need to take three months' rest." I stared at my doctor. *Three months' rest?* I thought. *With my commitments? My schedule? He can't be serious.*

He was speaking with me in his office. I was suffering from an acute case of chicken pox. On top of that, I was dealing with chronic fatigue and problems with my liver.

"Your physical condition has deteriorated significantly. You must rest if you hope to regain your health. In fact, here is my prescription." He handed me a piece of paper. On the paper, written in all capital letters, was:

REST!

While I did not take his advice at that time, he was right. I was on a road that would only lead to physical, emotional, and spiritual ruin. If I was to survive–much less thrive–I had to find a new way to live. But that would be easier said than done.

At the time, I had been General Secretary and CEO at Bangladesh Baptist Church Fellowship for 12 years. At age 30, I had been chosen to bring BBCF out of a deep hole, and had done so. I was deeply involved in leading and growing the ministry of my denomination. We had enjoyed many successes, for which I had received all of the credit. I also served on the boards of four major national ministries. I enjoyed a position of great prestige in my country–while also shouldering great responsibilities.

Getting free from the whirlwind of my life would take more than a few cosmetic changes. It would require a rethinking of who I was, how I lived, and how I led. And it would lead to me make changes that would run counter to powerful cultural patterns and traditions of my country.

THE ROAD TO SUCCESS—AND CRISIS

I WAS BORN AND raised in Bangladesh. Ours is a culture that promotes and honors the *guru* model of leadership. A strong person at the top holds great power. When successes are achieved, the guru gets all the credit. At the same time, it is expected of a guru to do everything on his or her own. With great power comes great obligation.

My upbringing prepared me to take on such a role. A third-generation Christian, my father had served in the Pakistani Air Force before coming back to East Pakistan (now Bangladesh) and a career in teaching. He first spent a few years with the New Zealand Baptist Missionary Society, then twenty years with the Red Crescent Society.

My father also served in key behind-the-scenes roles in his church, in administration and children's ministries. In the last two years of his life, he pastored a church that produced a number of leaders who went on to national influence in the Church in Bangladesh.

Ours was a disciplined family. My mother, who spent 42 years as a teacher, ran a buttoned-down household. Unlike most middle-class Bengali families who employed servants and maids, we did all of our own cleaning, cooking, shopping, gardening, and other household chores. We also did all of our own house maintenance, such as carpentry and electrical work. These chores were all subject to regular evening inspections. While my description might sound harsh, it was a wonderful discipline.

As I grew up, I was seen as a "good boy." I did well in school, attended church regularly, and was a leader in my youth group. But underneath my "good" exterior was a disturbed heart.

Bangladesh at that time was a very poor country. Even though we were considered middle-class, we lived a primitive life. We were lucky if we had meat once a month. Cookies and other sweets were the stuff of dreams. And a glass of cold water was a luxury.

At the same time, we lived among foreign missionaries. Their refrigerators, an appliance well beyond our financial reach, provided all the cold water they could drink.

Cookies and other baked goods were regular treats. And every day, they were feeding meat to their pet dogs!

These and other inequities created a deep resentment within me, although I hid it well from others. I continued on as a leader in the church youth group even as my resentment grew.

CONFRONTATION AND CHANGE

IN 1998, I VISITED the United States for the first time to attend a Youth Congress. That visit changed my worldview, particularly about Western culture and lifestyle.

Previously, I had resented the privileges enjoyed by the Western missionaries in Bangladesh. Now for the first time, I saw what these missionaries had given up to invest their lives in my country. Compared to the lifestyle they could have enjoyed had they stayed in America, they had chosen what for them was a life of simplicity, exposure to life-threatening disease, and having to cope with the challenges of navigating a country with limited infrastructure. I realized how much they had sacrificed to serve as missionaries in my country.

Upon returning to Bangladesh, I led a major youth conference. Even though my eyes had been opened during time in the United States, resentment still bubbled within me–and I began to act it out. At the conference, I intentionally wore a T-shirt with the words *"…and I don't care"* written on the back.

It was then that I was confronted by a senior pastor in my denomination. (Understand that direct confrontation is very unusual in my culture. In Bangladesh, communication is usually very roundabout, especially about sensitive issues.) "Leor," he said to me, "You have some problems with your attitude. There is something wrong. What is written on your T-shirt is what is written in your attitude.

"Leor, you have to care," he continued. "Even Jesus needed to get favor from the people. You need to make an effort to get favor from God and from the people." The pastor then quoted these words from Luke 2:52:

> *And Jesus grew in wisdom and stature, and
> in favor with God and man.*

The admonition from this pastor confirmed what I had been realizing: my attitude and my behavior needed to change. God began to work on my heart and my actions. These positive changes led to reconciliation with the missionaries and their associates.

It was the beginning of a major life change, a change that was happening at the same time that my leadership roles were continuing to increase.

FROM YOUTH LEADERSHIP TO DENOMINATIONAL CEO

BY NOW, IN ADDITION to leading my convention youth group, I was the youth secretary of the National Christian Fellowship of Bangladesh (a network of 19 evangelical and Pentecostal denominations and part of the World

Evangelical Alliance). This opportunity exposed me to many different denominations and Christian organizations. When the funds that supported my position ran out, I accepted a post with InterLife Bangladesh, a Swedish NGO committed to poverty alleviation, accessibility for disabled persons, and social justice. For two years, I worked at this disciplined, buttoned-down organization. At ILB, I received valuable management training. I learned how to handle authority, how to build accountability, how to handle resources, and more.

I was still a young man, just approaching thirty years of age. So imagine my shock when, out of nowhere, I was contacted by the senior leaders in my denomination, the Bangladesh Baptist Church Fellowship. These leaders wanted to talk to me about a position in the denomination–the CEO position.

I had no theological degree and no ordination. I considered myself totally unqualified to lead a church denomination filled with veteran pastors who held advanced theological degrees. In fact, I considered myself so unqualified that it never occurred to me that I would be a candidate.

Even more astounding, they were asking me to consider taking the position as a 30-year-old! Virtually anywhere in the world, a 30-year-old CEO would be considered unusual. But in my country, it is mind-boggling. Bangladesh is a culture that respects and reveres the elderly. Older age is a mark of maturity. Usually, a person is not even considered a mature adult until at least age 50.

"Why me?" I asked them when we met. "You know that I have no theological training, no ordination. And you know that I am a very young man. What makes you think that I would be qualified?"

They had answers. My positions in youth leadership, my own church convention, NCFB, and the Swedish NGO had proven my leadership capacity. And they actually viewed my youth as an asset. As a younger man, I could presumably serve longer in the position, providing stability.

There was another dynamic to the process, unique to my country. In 1971, East Pakistan fought a successful war of liberation with Pakistan and became Bangladesh. The leaders of the liberation movement became heroes in the country. These included the leaders of the Christian Church in Bangladesh.

As these heroes took on leadership roles in the government and in the Church, our elder-respecting culture embraced them for life. There was no thought that these leaders would eventually step down; they would hold their leadership positions for as long as they wished.

Their decades of service meant that a whole generation of potential leaders was disenfranchised. These leaders either left the country or withered away in middle-management roles. This lost generation of leadership created a gap in the flow of leaders in Bangladesh. At the time that I was approached to consider the General Secretary role, there were no leaders in the 40- to 50-year-old generation whom they felt could adequately fill the position.

After praying and consulting with my family, I accepted the invitation. In 2001, I assumed the position of Assistant General Secretary, and in 2002, I became General Secretary and CEO of the BBCF. Immediately upon my appointment, the pastor who had confronted me at the youth conference in 1998 was assigned to oversee the theological education that I did not yet have.

TAKING OVER A LEAKING BOAT

UPON TAKING THE position, I quickly learned that BBCF was on shaky ground. After decades of financial assistance from our three mission partners–the Australian, New Zealand, and US Baptist Conventions–support was withdrawn. We were now on our own to look after the 400+ churches that had been planted during a season of growth and outreach. We were also now responsible for all of our schools, children's homes, a hospital, and a multi-purpose training and conference facility.

In addition, relational problems and conflicts that had built up for years between the US and Bangladesh Conventions were coming to a head. And we were still dealing with the expulsion of the Australian Baptists from our country due to their Muslim outreach ministry.

But the biggest challenge I faced was the organization itself. BBCF had evolved in an era when the missionary/Bengali relationship resembled that of a parent to a child. Much of the interaction between missionaries and we locals consisted of handouts distributed by the missionaries. There was little to no accountability involved in these interactions. It was rare to keep records and do reporting. It was a loose charity system characteristic of Bangladeshi Christian organizations at that time.

This all had to change. Bringing my previous experience to bear, I began to build in reporting, planning, and accountability systems. The corporate culture of BBCF was wrenched from chaotic to competent, a painful process to say the least.

Gradually, these efforts began to reap fruit. Evangelists were now filing reports of their activities. We could track and respond to new believers and others who were drawn into our ministry. Our schools and hospitals were put on more stable footing. The *Prayer Garden*, our multi-purpose training facility, became profitable.

As General Secretary and CEO, I was functioning as a *guru*. I held all the power, was in charge of all of the tasks. I did everything, or at least it felt that way. And when things succeeded, I took all of the credit. The efforts of my staff went unnoticed as my reputation and credibility continued to grow.

By 2011, I was becoming a leader of national impact, considered one of the top Christian leaders in Bangladesh. If I called, people would come running–from all denominations, and even from the Catholic Church. I had reached the top.

HITTING THE WALL

THE REALITY WAS, however, that I was headed down a deep hole. I was struggling spiritually, literally losing my connection with God. My pride began to get out of control. I was taking on an ever-increasing list of responsibilities and commitments and had little time for my wife and family. There was no balance in my life.

Despite all of my success, things were not smooth with my colleagues in BBCF. "There is a problem," I was told by that same pastor who had confronted me so many years ago. "A group of middle-aged leaders resent that you are holding the top position at such a young age." The pastor shared Paul's words of encouragement from 1 Timothy 4:12 (*Don't let anyone look down on you because you are young, but set an example for the believers in speech, in conduct, in love, in faith, and in purity*), but they provided only limited comfort.

The situation was aggravated by conflicts that were arising with leaders of the organizations on which I served as a board member. Unlike most people in my culture, I often speak my mind. If I see something that I don't like, I will say something about it. In my role as a board member, I was doing just this sort of speaking out, to the consternation of the organizational leaders. Anger and mistrust grew as our conflicts increased.

All of this began to take its toll. My health deteriorated. I contracted a severe case of the chicken pox, right in the middle of Bangladesh's hottest season. I suffered from chronic fatigue. I was losing interest in my work, my accomplishments, everything. And now, my doctor was telling me that I had to take three months' rest. Impossible! But try as I might to fight against it, I had hit the wall. Something would have to change.

Finally in 2014, God intervened. A Canadian partner offered me an opportunity to work with a life coach. "If you are willing, Leor," he told me, "you can meet with the coach and check him out. If you decide that you want to continue with him, we will underwrite the costs."

I agreed to give it a try. The coach came over to Bangladesh. We had two sessions together. And my life began to change.

The relationship with my coach has been a turning point for me. He does not suggest solutions or give me game plans. He listens, asks great questions, and constantly reminds me that I have to find the solutions for my situation. This is the process I have been in for the past two years and it continues to this day.

SEARCHING FOR SOLUTIONS...
SPARKING A REVOLUTION

"For my thoughts are not your thoughts,
neither are your ways my ways,"
declares the LORD.

"As the heavens are higher than the earth,
so are my ways higher than your ways
and my thoughts than your thoughts."

Isaiah 55:8-9

SEARCHING FOR SOLUTIONS has led to a revolution in my approach to life, to ministry, and to my world. I have realized that my priorities must be as follows: first, my relationship with God; second, my relationship with my family; and third, ministry and other responsibilities.

I have invested more time and heart into my love relationship with Jesus, and my spiritual life has improved. My family now has permission to confront me directly when my schedule keeps me away from home too often. (This kind of permission is very unusual in our culture.)

My emotional capacity and physical energy have improved as I have cut back on my commitments, including resigning from all four of the major ministry boards upon which I had been serving. I have become willing to sacrifice some of my prestige for the sake of balance and health.

But it is at BBCF where some of the most significant changes have been made. I have made a choice to put down the guru model of leadership and invest in our team. This investment involves changing how I relate to my team, trying to live out Paul's words about the example shown to us by Jesus himself:

In your relationships with one another,
have the same mindset as Christ Jesus:
Who, being in very nature God,
did not consider equality with God something to be
used to his own advantage;
rather, he made himself nothing
by taking the very nature of a servant,
being made in human likeness.
And being found in appearance as a man,
he humbled himself
by becoming obedient to death–
even death on a cross!

Philippians 2:5-8

I am learning to appreciate my staff, and to show them my appreciation. I am releasing power, delegating responsibilities, and giving my staff the authority to implement their ideas. Most important of all, I am sharing the credit for our collective accomplishments. Rather than trying to continually enhance my reputation, my prayer is that I can lead through the way that I live. I want my life to serve as the primary model for my leadership. I am happy when my colleagues can receive the credit they so richly deserve for the contributions they are making.

My sense of calling has shifted–from building the organization to identifying and discipling emerging leaders. When I am in our churches and at our denominational events, I am looking for men and women in whom I sense the gifting and potential to become transformational leaders for Christ. As I identify them, I begin to build relationships with them and get to know them better.

When God helps me to discern those who are truly called to leadership, I begin a mentoring process. I help them to understand their potential for leadership. I seek to create opportunities for these younger leaders to assume positions of responsibility and leadership within the ministry. I invest in Bible training with these leaders, helping them to deepen their understanding of the Word and how God's truths apply to their lives and the lives of their flocks.

Ultimately, I am hoping to model through my life what the journey of discipleship can look like. Spending time with these leaders not only exposes them to me, but me to them. They get to know me, learn my strengths and weaknesses, and (I pray) see how God is at work in and through me, day by day, to form a growing Christ follower walking more deeply in relationship with him.

BIG CHANGES, BIG BENEFITS

THESE CHANGES HAVE already reaped gratifying benefits. Younger leaders are drawn to me as they sense permission to stretch and grow in their lives and ministries. The model of my experience is inspiring other organizations to raise up younger leaders in their midst.

This recruitment of younger leaders is crucial because we face a major challenge in Bangladesh–competition with the business world, high-paying professions, and even "business as ministry" for the allegiance of promising younger leaders. The Church in Bangladesh is losing many of its veteran leaders as the stalwarts from the Class of 1971 succumb to retirement and death. We must attract these gifted younger leaders if the Church is to survive and grow.

An exciting new model for ministry that is emerging from this revolution is training pastors as couples. We are now training couples as one unit, a pastoral family. Women have a vital role in ministry; this training approach enables these women to maximize their role and their effectiveness as they minister alongside their spouses. And in terms of evangelism, women are able to reach other women and families in ways that men cannot.

LOOKING TO THE FUTURE:
PLANNING FOR SUCCESSION AND BEYOND

AT THIS WRITING, I am 44 years old—still quite young by most standards. But it is clear that planning for long-term succession must begin now. We must fight against the cultural pattern that runs so strongly through Bangladesh society: the model of "leader for life." So often, leaders in our country remain in place until they die, leaving a leadership vacuum that usually results in chaos.

I am determined that this will not happen to BBCF. At this writing, we are preparing to send a group of leaders to the Philippines for advanced theological and ministry education. After five years, we hope that God will raise up someone from the group whom we discern the Lord has chosen to be my successor. I can then begin the process of grooming this person for the role as we plan for the future transition.

Time will tell as to how our hopes, dreams, and plans will evolve. As we know, the future can hold many surprises. But I am trusting God that, as he has enabled me to envision and implement the revolution of these past few years, he will empower me and my colleagues in ministry to discern the best ways to move forward. I am grateful that God is using my experiences as a young leader to inspire other Christian organizations in my country to pursue a counter-cultural paradigm for the sake of the kingdom. And I am especially grateful that the Lord has given me a vision for leadership that is not only effective, but is nurturing for my family, my health, and my soul.

"Therefore go and make disciples of all nations, baptizing them in the name of the Father and of the Son and of the Holy Spirit, and teaching them to obey everything I have commanded you. And surely I am with you always, to the very end of the age."

Matthew 28:19-20

A man may do an immense deal of good, if he does not care who gets the credit for it.

Father Strickland, Jesuit Priest, UK, 1863

The Blasphemy of "Worship"

A Call for a New Paradigm

ADRIAN DE VISSER

For many years as a believer, I struggled to understand the significance of or the necessity for worship. I saw others enjoy worshiping the Lord, but I did it because it was required of me. If I were given a choice, I would rather be active doing something for the Lord than be at his feet. I honestly took pride in the fact that I worked very hard for the Lord (little did I realize I was hiding behind activity to cover my insecurities).

My deep struggle began with the question: Why does God need my worship? At times I concluded that God was very egocentric to demand my worship. Tormented by my own thoughts, I rejected this position; but soon, I concluded that worship was something we humans created on our own to fill needs in our own hearts. Furthermore, I assumed that it was not essential for me.

A STRUGGLE SHARED

AN ENCOUNTER WITH C. S. Lewis's book *Reflections on the Psalms* made me aware that I was not alone in my struggle. In the book, Lewis recounts the problems he had with many of the psalms–namely, that God so often calls people to praise him. Lewis says, "We all despise the man who demands continued assurance of his own virtue, intelligence or delightfulness" (p. 77). He continues, "It was hideously like saying, 'What I most want is to be told that I am good and great'" (p. 78).

Lewis reflected on why we praise anything at all. What do we mean, for example, when we say that a picture, a piece of music, or a book is "admirable"? We mean that people ought to admire those things, and if they do not, they will lose out and miss something wonderful. This began to help Lewis understand the calls to praise God. If God is the great object of admiration behind all other beauties and magnificence, then to praise and admire him would be "simply to be awake, to have entered the real world" (p. 79). Not doing so would be to become far more profoundly crippled than those who are blind, deaf, and bedridden.

That was not all Lewis discovered. "The most obvious fact about praise–whether of God or anything–strangely escaped me" (p. 80). He had never noticed that all enjoyment spontaneously overflows into praise unless "shyness or the fear of boring others is deliberately brought in to check it" (p. 80). When you find anything great or enthralling, you have an almost visceral, instinctive need to praise it to others and get others to recognize it. "Listen to this," you say to your friend. "I can't wait for you to read it. You'll absolutely love it. Isn't it great? Isn't it wonderful?" (cf. p. 81). Why, when we have had our imaginations captured by something, do we unavoidably need to do this? Lewis answered, "I think we delight to praise what we enjoy because the praise not merely expresses but completes the enjoyment; it is its appointed consummation" (p. 81).

A FRESH UNDERSTANDING OF WORSHIP

LEWIS'S INSIGHTS LED ME on a new journey. Perhaps my skepticism toward worship came out of an inadequate understanding of God's love and an inadequate understanding of the depth of my alienation from him and his sacrificial love of redemption.

God created me in his own image. By this act he offered me worth and significance (Genesis 1:26-27). He created a beautiful world and invited me to enjoy it and also rule over it (Genesis 1:28-30). He created me a little below himself (Psalm 8:5-6). The word *elohim* can mean angelic creatures (see Hebrews 2:7), but here it definitely means God. The Lord crowned Adam and Eve and gave them dominion over the other creatures (Genesis 1:26-27). We are co-regents of creation with the Lord! The angels are servants (Hebrews 1:14), but we are kings. One day, all who have trusted Christ will be like him (1 John 3:1-3, Romans 8:29).

When I messed up, his love for me was so great that he sent his only begotten Son to die for me. Even as I meditate on this truth, I find myself humming the tune, "Amazing Grace." This is worship: the redeemed of the Lord, acknowledging the greatness of God, expressing our gratitude for his love and the hope he has offered to us. This is more than just a speech or something said repeatedly and ritualistically.

Worship is about being so impressed by the character of God, so influenced by his marvelous attributes, that we have to say *something*. We are compelled by the sheer power and majesty of the Lord to bless him or praise his name. We cannot contain our adoration for him! His Word has reached our hearts and had the intended influence.

This fresh understanding of worship transformed my personal love relationship with God. But this transformation collided with my experience with much of what is termed "worship" in our modern churches.

"WORSHIP" AS ENTERTAINMENT

MUCH OF WORSHIP TODAY has become mere entertainment for people. We are not worshiping God; rather, we have become spectators who attend services expecting to be entertained. To call this *worship* is disrespectful and demeaning toward God. Worship to God is holy and sacred. To pervert it into an entertainment experience designed for our benefit is nothing short of blasphemy.

We have failed to empower men and women who are in deep love with the Lord to lead the church in worship. Rather, we have empowered men and women to lead worship based on their musical abilities and vocal talents. "I am what I love," Augustine said. Our most fundamental identity and life behavior is a function of what we love. Musicians love music; they will produce good music. Good worship leaders, on the other hand, love the Lord. This enables them to lead people into worship and praise.

We operate under the erroneous concept that worship must be attractive to the audience. While there is a degree of legitimacy to this concept, I suggest that when we come together for worship, we come to worship Holy God, not to entertain people. We invest in the quality of our worship because God deserves our best, not because worship should be a means to attract people to the church. When we go down that track, we turn the church into place of entertainment rather than a temple of worship.

But here in Sri Lanka and throughout Asia, there is an additional wrinkle. The modern "worship" entertainment experience reflects a Western perspective on what is worship–or more crassly put, a Western perspective on what is entertaining. The flow, pace, musical and artistic expressions, and the energy of the worship experience itself, all emanate out of a Western context. For the Asian– especially from Buddhist, Hindu, or Islamic contexts–this creates a jarring cultural collision.

ETHNOCENTRISM AND ITS IMPACT ON WORSHIP

THE EARLY MISSIONARIES who ministered in my part of the world approached our cultures with the presumption that they were totally evil. To embrace Christianity also required a complete rejection of one's culture. In Sri Lanka, which lived under the colonial yoke for centuries, this ethos was legislated into our society through a 1711 law which stated that Christians participating in the "ceremonies of heathenism" would be liable to a public whipping and imprisonment in irons for one year.

The early missionaries then introduced "authentic" Christian worship–Western forms that were alien to our cultures. In doing so, they cemented the impression of Christianity as an inherently foreign religion in the hearts and minds of millions of unreached people in Asia. (This imposition of a Western cultural model for the Christian faith could have much to do with why, after hundreds of years of sincere outreach conducted by dedicated Christ followers, the Christian community in countries like Sri Lanka still comprises a tiny minority of the population.)

So how do we break out of our self-created cultural bubbles? If we are going to regain both an understanding of what is authentic worship, and how authentic worship translates across cultures, it is important that we first understand the concepts of worship already existent in the indigenous cultures we hope to reach.

AN ASIAN EXAMPLE: BUDDHISM

MY COUNTRY, SRI LANKA, is predominantly Buddhist. Buddhists dress in white to attend the temple for worship. They take off their shoes or slippers before entering the temple. There is no shouting or even whispering within the place of worship. At all times, they conduct themselves as if they are in the presence of an all-powerful god. Young and old, rich and poor alike, they sit on the floor, chant their prayers, and listen to the preacher with absolute reverence.

Let's compare the Buddhist approach to worship with what is common in many churches, including here in Sri Lanka. In all honesty, our worship can look and feel like a musical entertainment show. Lights dazzle, smoke bursts, drums bang, music pounds. The main actors are the worship team and the worshipers; God himself is sidelined. To the Buddhist, this high-energy cacophony is not only inappropriate to worship, it is demeaning and worldly.

As I write these words, I can already envision the protests I will get from my Western and African friends. They will point out that the Bible says we are to rejoice before the Lord. I am aware that David danced before the Lord, and I can quote Scriptures that tell us to shout unto the Lord. But can I also quote 1 Corinthians 8:9: *Be careful, however, that the exercise of your freedom does not become a stumbling block to the weak.*

My point is not that all nations should follow one form of worship, or that the Asian form of worship is better than that of the rest of the world. What I am suggesting is that, *in each context, we seek to develop forms of worship that are culturally appropriate to the people we are trying to reach.* We should endeavor to craft our worship, especially when connecting with unreached peoples, in the spirit of Paul's entreaty to the Corinthians:

*Though I am free and belong to no one, I have made myself
a slave to everyone, to win as many as possible. To the Jews
I became like a Jew, to win the Jews. To those under the law
I became like one under the law (though I myself am not
under the law), so as to win those under the law. To those not
having the law I became like one not having the law (though
I am not free from God's law but am under Christ's law), so
as to win those not having the law. To the weak I became
weak, to win the weak. I have become all things to all people
so that by all possible means I might save some. I do all this
for the sake of the gospel, that I may share in its blessings.*

1 Corinthians 9:19-23

WORSHIP: A BIBLICAL CONTEXT

TO CRAFT APPROACHES to worship appropriate to particular cultural contexts, we will first need to gain a fundamental understanding of the biblical view of worship. Worship is God-centered, not human-centered. When we worship to please God instead of ourselves, then and only then will our worship be meaningful and spiritually uplifting to us, and acceptable to God.

Changing our fundamental understanding of and approach to worship is a big undertaking, because we have all developed our own cultures of worship. But I invite you to join me in studying worship in the Old and New Testaments. I will then conclude by suggesting some areas that need our attention.

Worship In The Old Testament

THE MOST COMMON WORD used in the Old Testament for worship is the word *shaha* (bow down)–to prostate oneself before another in order to bestow honor and reverence (Genesis 22:5). This mode of salutation consisted in falling upon one's knees, then touching one's forehead to the ground (Genesis 19:1; 42:6; 48:12; 1 Samuel 25:41). *Shaha* is used specifically to refer to bowing down before God, to worship rendered to God, and also to false gods (Genesis 22:5; Exodus 24:1; 33:10; Judges 7:15; Job 1:20; Psalm 22:27; 86:9).

The word *worship* in the Old Testament describes the reverential attitude of mind, body, or both, combined with the notions of religious adoration, obedience, and service.

Components Of Old Testament Worship

Public Worship

General public worship, especially as developed in the Temple services, consisted of:

- sacrificial acts, when the blood of the offerings flowed in lavish profusion;

- ceremonial acts of reverence or adoration, symbolizing the seeking and receiving of the divine favor;

- public prayer, such as is described in Deuteronomy 26, at the dedication of the Temple (2 Chronicles 6), or as written in Psalm 79;

- praise by the official ministrants of the people–instrumental, vocal, or both; and

- singing, as a significant part of temple worship (2 Chronicles 5:12-13; 30:21; Nehemiah 12:27)–a whole company of priests were dedicated to the specific purpose of singing praise to God.

Private Worship

It appears that regular worship ceased when the Temple was destroyed and the Israelites were taken captive to Babylon. During this time, we have a record mostly of people's private worship. Daniel's habit of praying three times a day is a famous example of this (Daniel 6:10).

Private worship was not a new thing; it had precedent in the Psalms and elsewhere. The devout exiles were carrying on a tradition of private worship without the accompanying form of corporate worship. Often, their prayers look forward to the restoration of the Jews to their land, addressing God as "the God who keeps his covenant" and confessing the sins that brought about the Babylonian captivity (Nehemiah 1; Ezra 10; Daniel 9).

Confession

Solomon's prayer in 2 Chronicles 6 (particularly verses 36-39) makes it clear that confession of sin was a significant aspect of prayer and worship. We find both Nehemiah and Ezra privately confessing sin at the beginning of their books, and we have a beautiful prayer of confession recorded in Daniel.

Later on, when Ezra and Nehemiah are dealing with a particular problem of the Jews marrying pagan wives, there is a time of public confession of sin (Ezra 9-10) where the people get right with God again.

Public confession of sin has happened in revivals throughout history up to this day. It is the way God's attitude toward his people is turned from wrath to favor. Notice also that the prayers of confession in the Bible are not merely for the sins of the individual but also for the sins of the fathers and even the nation as a whole.

Reading of the Law

> Ezra opened the book. All the people could see him because he was standing above them; and as he opened it, the people all stood up. Ezra praised the LORD, the great God; and all the people lifted their hands and responded, "Amen! Amen!" Then they bowed down and worshiped the LORD with their faces to the ground.

> The Levites–Jeshua, Bani, Sherebiah, Jamin, Akkub, Shabbethai, Hodiah, Maaseiah, Kelita, Azariah, Jozabad, Hanan and Pelaiah–instructed the people in the Law while the people were standing there. They read from the Book of the Law of God, making it clear and giving the meaning so that the people understood what was being read.

> Nehemiah 8:5-8

IN AN AGE WHEN books required the skins of several animals and the painstaking handwriting of a scribe, not many people had their own copy of God's Word. Yet every man needed to know God's Word because it was the very foundation of worship and life. Therefore, the reading of the Scriptures was a very important part of corporate worship. Moses commanded that the entirety of the law be read to every man, woman, and child in Israel every seven years (Deuteronomy 31:9-12). Through these readings, the people were familiarized with God's Word.

Tradition has it that the *Targums* were developed later on as the reading of the Scriptures was carried on during the exile. The Targums were loose translations of the Hebrew Scriptures into Aramaic, the language of the common people at that time. It is believed that this is what Nehemiah meant when he describes the worship service held by the returned exiles in which they read the Scriptures:

> *They read from the Book of the Law of God, making it clear and giving the meaning so that the people understood what was being read.*
>
> *Nehemiah 8:8*

Prostration

WHENEVER THE BIBLE describes what people are doing when they worship, three things are consistent:

- They are near the thing they are worshiping–"before God," "in God's holy mountain," or in front of an idol.

- They are offering sacrifices.

- They are bowing (2 Chronicles 20:18; Nehemiah 8:6).

Meditation

"Christian meditation is a form of prayer in which a structured attempt is made to become aware of and reflect upon the revelations of God. The word *meditation* comes from the Latin word *meditārī*, which has a range of meanings including to reflect on, to study and to practice."[2]

Meditation is referred to throughout the Old Testament as an act of worship–deliberate, close, and continuous (Psalms 1:2; 119:97). The worshiper is encouraged to meditate on aspects like the works of creation (Psalms 19:1-6); the perfections of God (Deuteronomy 32:4); the dispensations of Providence (Psalms 97:1-2); and the precepts and promises of God's words (Psalms 119).

Worship In the New Testament

IN THE NEW TESTAMENT, the principal word for worship (used 59 times) is *proskuneo*–"kiss (the hand or the ground) toward." In Asian cultures, this would be expressed by bowing prostrate upon the ground.

Proskuneu can be used to refer to rendering homage to men, angels, demons, the Devil, the "beast," idols, or to God. It is used 16 times to refer to Jesus as a beneficent superior, and at least 24 times to God or to Jesus as God. It is always translated worship. Worship in this context suggests humans acknowledging the greatness of God while realizing their own inadequacies: falling down before God and acknowledging him as Lord.

The first uses of *worship* and *worshiped* in the New Testament are in Matthew chapter 2, verses 2, 8, and 11. In verse 2, the wise men are looking for the One born King of the Jews in order to worship him. In verse 8, Herod states he wants to worship him also. Worshiping does not occur in these two verses. It does occur in verse 11: *"They bowed down and worshiped him."*

Here we see that the first worshiping in the New Testament incorporated a *falling down* or *bowing.* When the wise men fell down (or bowed), they acknowledged the superiority of the Child and his sovereignty over them.

The Worship/Service Connection

THE NEXT OCCURRENCE of worship in the New Testament is in Matthew 4:9-10. The Devil offers Jesus all the kingdoms of the world and their glories if Jesus will bow down and worship him. Hence, again, falling or bowing is an element of worship.

Jesus answers the Devil in verse 10, saying only God is to be worshiped and only he is to be served. From this, we can conclude that proper worship–that which is acceptable to God–requires the element of serving him, that is, being submissive to him.

A Worship Paradigm Shift

LET US CONSIDER John 4:7-26, the encounter of Jesus and a woman in Samaria. The woman knows Jesus is a Jew, and that Jews do not associate with Samaritans. The woman concludes Jesus is a prophet and points out the conflict between Samaritans and Jews regarding worship (verse 20).

Prophetically, Jesus tells the woman of a change that is going to take place in the whole arena of worshiping God. Jesus tells her that God is a "spirit" and those who worship him must do so in "spirit and in truth."

What is he telling her? What is the change that is to take place?

The seat of worshiping God for the Jews was Jerusalem– at the temple. Worshiping also involved the physical: physical sacrifices, physical offerings, and the physical presence of the priests. Worshiping God for the Jews was restricted to the Temple.

Hence, was not Jesus referring to how all this would change with the birth of the Church–the commencing of the body of Christ? With the indwelling of the Holy Spirit, God now dwells in each believer. His presence is no longer limited to the Temple. Each believer is now a priest, and worship is no longer confined to specific events, activities, or locations.

What the New Testament tells us (and does not tell us) about Worship

After carefully considering the New Testament passages related to worship, I am forced to conclude:

1. The New Testament does not contain any passage that allows us to define what constitutes worship for the Church on Earth. From the Greek words, we see the specific act of bowing down or falling to prostration as being worship, whether directed to (before) Jesus, God, idols, or the beast(s). Note the same root word is used regardless of the object of worship.

2. With respect to the Jews worshiping in the Temple in Jerusalem, we see that worship took place, but the New Testament does not provide any details of their worship, other than bowing or rendering homage.

3. No reference to worshiping God and Jesus taking place in heaven indicates anything other than bowing or prostration and confession (admission) as the consummation of worship.

4. No specific instruction is given to the Church to worship her Lord or to worship God. Also, there is no instruction regarding worshiping the Holy Spirit, or a record of anyone worshiping him.

Therefore, what we may have believed to be worship and what we may have prescribed as worship may not have any substantiation in Scripture. Furthermore, if we insist on a particular worship formula or mode, we are establishing our own standards for worship, not standards from the Bible.

But since worship and worship services are so universal throughout the Church, must there not be some scriptural enjoinment for its existence? What are the bases for what we do when we gather together? What should we do? What should we not do?

TRANSFORMATION AS AN EXPRESSION OF WORSHIP

PAUL, IN HIS LETTER to the believers in Rome, presents the arguments and rationale for the superiority of faith in Christ as that which brings deliverance. This was to supersede the previous deliverance Israel obtained thru the Law of Moses.

Under the Law, righteousness was obtained by obeying the Law and offering sacrifices. But the sacrifice of Christ has put aside the sacrifices required under the Law, and the righteousness of Christ is now imparted (imputed) to the believer–not because of his obedience to the Law–but because of his faith in Christ (Romans 1-11).

Because of all of this, Paul urges the believer (12:1) to present his own body as a living sacrifice, holy and acceptable (well pleasing) to God, and continues to state that doing so is nothing less than being reasonable in serving God. Although this is not a requirement for our deliverance (salvation), it does cause us to realize the somberness of what we can do with our bodies.

Paul goes on (12:2) to state the means of doing so: by not being conformed to the behavior and conduct patterns of the world (this age), but rather to be transformed by the renewing of our minds (understanding). Perhaps a more accurate translation would be: allow yourselves to be transformed. Hence, although it does not require action, it implies submission on the part of the one undergoing the transformation.

It has the root *metamorfow*, which means: to change one's form, to be transfigured. The same root occurs in Matthew 17:2 and in Mark 9:2, in which Christ is transfigured.

We can conclude that this transformation is accomplished by God (Holy Spirit), and our submission to his will is through our spiritual nature.

Is not our wanting God to transform us more in keeping with what worship is than our weekly worship services within the context of our local church?

WORSHIP AND THE INDWELLING OF THE HOLY SPIRIT

THE UNIQUE CHARACTERISTIC that makes the church different from all other bodies of believers is that her members are indwelled by the Holy Spirit. In 1 Corinthians, Paul teaches that the body of the believer is a temple of God (3:16). Our bodies are also members of Christ; hence, a believer must not ever join his or her body with that of a prostitute, or be sexually immoral, because the body is the temple of the Holy Spirit (6:15-19).

- Since our bodies are temples of God, can we gather for worship in any building or place that is a more appropriate "temple"?

- Since our bodies are continuously temples of the Holy Spirit (God), can we ask him to meet with us when we gather to worship?

- Since our bodies are continuously temples of the Holy Spirit (God), can we leave him at the church when the worship service ends?

- Since our bodies are continuously temples of the Holy Spirit (God), are we not in a sense the temple keepers?

THE ELEMENT OF PRAISE

Through Jesus, therefore, let us continually offer to God a sacrifice of praise–the fruit of lips that openly profess his name.

Hebrews 13:15

HERE IS ANOTHER spiritual sacrifice which pleases God– praising and thanking him for all that he is and all that he does for us.

The practice of thankfulness to God is stressed over and over again in the New Testament (e.g., 1 Thessalonians 5:16-18; Colossians 3:15-17). Why is this? Does God need our gratitude so that he can feel good about himself?

Such a view does not befit the God of the Bible–he is the only being in the universe who is completely self-existent and therefore needs nothing. We add nothing to God by praising and thanking him. God is indeed pleased by our gratitude, but the ones who benefit from this practice are us!

As we choose to recall God's blessings and then to thank him for these, we are keeping ourselves properly aligned with reality. Rather than buying into the lie that we are mistreated and unfortunate, we are by faith asserting the truth–that we are fantastically blessed beyond anything we could ever deserve.

The author's emphasis here is that we should worship God in this way continually. The idea that Christian worship takes place only in a corporate worship meeting is foreign to the writer of Hebrews. Because of Christ's payment for our sins, we have the privilege to draw near to God and communicate to him in this way at any time: in the morning when we wake up, on the way to work, during our busy day, when we are together with other Christians, alone in our room–anywhere.

GENEROSITY AS WORSHIP

And do not forget to do good and to share with others, for with such sacrifices God is pleased.

Hebrews 13:16

THE AUTHOR OF HEBREWS touches on two more ways in which we can worship God: doing good and sharing. *Sharing* refers to the generous giving of our material resources to God's people and God's work. This is explicitly identified by Paul as a sacrifice which pleases God: *But I have received [your money gift] in full, and have an abundance; I am amply supplied, having received from Epaphroditus what you have sent, a fragrant aroma, an acceptable sacrifice, well-pleasing to God* (Philippians 4:18).

Many Christians regard giving financially to God in the same way that they pay their taxes to the government: they look for ways to give as little as possible. Paul's view is very different from this. He says that giving is a privilege (2 Corinthians 8:4) and something that we should do generously (2 Corinthians 9:6), as an expression of our commitment to God (2 Corinthians 8:5).

When we give our money to God by supporting our local church, other Christian workers and ministries, and helping the needy, God regards this as an expression of worship, fully as spiritual as praising him. This is because the giving of our money represents a giving of ourselves, since money represents the time and effort and creativity that we have invested in order to gain it. Such giving is also an expression of our trust in God's faithfulness to continue to meet our material needs–which Paul tells us God will fully supply (Philippians 4:19).

SERVICE AS WORSHIP

THE OTHER SACRIFICE mentioned in this verse is doing good. This phrase refers to ministry–performing deeds of loving service to other people as a representative of Christ. When we relate to the people God brings into our lives with Christ-like, sacrificial love, God regards this as an expression of our worship to him: *Walk in the way of love, just as Christ loved us and gave himself up for us as a fragrant offering and sacrifice to God (Ephesians 5:1-2).*

God is pleased by this kind of life not only because he wants to love people through us, but also because this demonstrates that we are living with an attitude of trust in his love for us. We are motivated to love others because we understand and believe in the love that God has for us (1 John 4:16-19).

Every day, God gives us dozens of creative opportunities to worship him through our service: serving our spouses, caring for our children, performing deeds of service for those in need, sharing the love of Christ with our neighbors or those at work or at school–the examples are endless.

EXERCISING OUR SPIRITUAL GIFTS AS WORSHIP

WE ALSO HAVE THE privilege to worship God through the exercise of our spiritual gifts. Paul speaks of his own apostolic ministry in this way: *I have written you quite boldly...because of the grace God gave me to be a minister of Christ Jesus to the Gentiles. He gave me the priestly duty of proclaiming the gospel of God, so that the Gentiles might become an offering acceptable to God, sanctified by the Holy Spirit* (Romans 15:15-16).

After urging us to present our lives to God as an act of worship in Romans 12:1, Paul goes on to urge us to express that worship through the use of our spiritual gifts (12:6-8). As we discover our spiritual gifts, exercise them regularly in the service of others, and give God praise for the fruit of this ministry, we discover a form of worship that is uniquely satisfying!

THE CENTRALITY OF JUSTICE IN WORSHIP

Hear the word of the Lord,
you rulers of Sodom;

listen to the instruction of our God,
you people of Gomorrah!

"The multitude of your sacrifices—
what are they to me?" says the Lord.

"I have more than enough of burnt offerings,
of rams and the fat of fattened animals;

I have no pleasure
in the blood of bulls and lambs and goats.

When you come to appear before me,
who has asked this of you,
this trampling of my courts?

Stop bringing meaningless offerings!
Your incense is detestable to me.

New Moons, Sabbaths and convocations—
I cannot bear your worthless assemblies.

Your New Moon feasts and your appointed festivals
I hate with all my being.

They have become a burden to me;
I am weary of bearing them.

Isaiah 1:10-14

WHY WAS GOD so angry with his people that he refused to accept their worship? What did God expect from them? Verses 16 and 17 provide the answer:

Wash and make yourselves clean.
Take your evil deeds out of my sight;
stop doing wrong.
Learn to do right; seek justice.
Defend the oppressed. Take up the cause of the fatherless;
plead the case of the widow.

Only when they dealt with the evils of injustice did God assure His people that he would forgive their sins. Unfortunately, we have ignored the context and use this verse in evangelistic settings to offer people the assurance of God's forgiveness.

WORSHIP: MUCH MORE THAN A SERVICE

IT SHOULD BE CLEAR from this study that worship is a lifestyle made up of many components rather than some sort of periodic, corporate meeting.

Why is this important? When we have a superficial view of what worship is, the result is a superficial and dichotomized Christian life. We may faithfully attend our Sunday worship service, but because we view that as the essence of worship, we fail to develop a lifestyle of wholehearted commitment to God, an attitude of thankfulness, a commitment to financial stewardship, and a lifestyle of ministry. God is more pleased, and we are more fulfilled, when we develop lifestyles characterized by the fully-orbed worship described in the Old and New Testaments.

DEVELOPING A BIBLICAL, CULTURALLY-RELEVANT LIFESTYLE OF WORSHIP

I BELIEVE THAT Isaiah 6:1-8 can serve as a template to articulate the characteristics of a biblical lifestyle of worship capable of being contextualized for any cultural environment:

In the year that King Uzziah died, I saw the Lord, high and exalted, seated on a throne; and the train of his robe filled the temple. Above him were seraphim, each with six wings: With two wings they covered their faces, with two they covered their feet, and with two they were flying. And they were calling to one another:

*"Holy, holy, holy is the Lord Almighty;
the whole earth is full of his glory."*

At the sound of their voices the doorposts and thresholds shook and the temple was filled with smoke.

"Woe to me!" I cried. "I am ruined! For I am a man of unclean lips, and I live among a people of unclean lips, and my eyes have seen the King, the Lord Almighty."

Then one of the seraphim flew to me with a live coal in his hand, which he had taken with tongs from the altar. With it he touched my mouth and said, "See, this has touched your lips; your guilt is taken away and your sin atoned for."

Then I heard the voice of the Lord saying, "Whom shall I send? And who will go for us?"

And I said, "Here am I. Send me!"

Worship begins with a revelation of Almighty God (6:1-2). It is followed by proclaiming the holiness of God with deep reverence (6:3). The dramatic tumult in verse 4 attests to God's approval of their worship. Our natural reaction to this intense proximity to holiness ought to be confession (6:5), immediately followed by God's swift dispensation of forgiveness (6:6). Finally, the call to live out our faith in grateful response to God's gift of grace and forgiveness is made by God, and accepted by us (6:7-8).

TRUE WORSHIP

THIS IS NOT ENTERTAINMENT. This is true worship. Its expression can take many forms–each form appropriate to its specific cultural context. The forms can be particular; the underlying truth is universal.

My prayer is that, as we are called by God to reach out to those who have never been introduced to him or to his saving gospel, we will joyfully let go of our own cultural baggage and, with freedom, adapt the universal truths of God's worship to connect with those lost men, women, and children, all of whom are deeply loved by our Creator. Amen.

---

[2] Christian meditation - *https://en.wikipedia.org/wiki/Christian_meditation*

Bringing the Bible to Life

Freeing Bible Teaching from the Bonds of Culture

PETER DEBAKAR MAZUMDER

My back was killing me. Trying to sit up in my chair, I struggled to pay attention to the speaker. *How much longer is this going to go on?* I thought. *He has been speaking for two hours, and there is no sign that he is nearing the end.*

The speaker had a reputation as a respected preacher and Bible teacher. Based on his credentials, I had booked him to deliver the main message at our student conference. But my experience with him leading up to the conference had been nothing but frustration. I had repeatedly sent him information on the theme we wished him to address, but never received a reply or acknowledgment that he had received my emails.

When he arrived at the conference, his first words to me were, "What do you want me to speak on?" He brushed off my alarmed look. "Don't worry. I need only a little time to prepare. I will be ready to deliver my message." And deliver he did–for *two and a half hours*.

Instead of teaching on the topic that we had asked him to address (or any topic at all), he presented random thoughts, using bits and pieces from various passages in the Bible. We realized that not only had he not prepared in advance, he had not prepared at all. In fact, he was not even aware of the main theme for the conference.

His talk, twice as long as we had requested, disrupted the schedule for the rest of the day. Beyond that, his teaching had no impact. He delivered Bible truths–but in a dry, abstract way. There was no heart connection, nothing compelling in the intellectual concepts he presented. Worst of all, he provided no practical application from the Scriptures. He offered no suggestions for how the truths he shared from the Bible could be applied. Our students walked out of his session with nothing that they could use for their own lives.

WANTED: COMPELLING BIBLE TEACHERS

I WISH I COULD tell you that my experience with this pastor was an aberration. But in my country, Bangladesh, there is a shortage of pastors and leaders who are able to teach the Bible in a compelling way.

The Scriptures are taught–but the presentations are too often mechanical and wooden. Many times, pastors will simply read a Bible passage, then close the Scriptures and talk about any number of unrelated topics. Their commentary often has little to do with the Scripture read; the reading of the Word is done more to satisfy a ceremonial expectation than to provide solid teaching. And this ritual is often taken by the congregation as the way that they should approach Scripture in their personal reading. These mechanical, rote, and even off-base presentations of Scripture mean that though people do hear from God's Word, it does not reach their hearts.

The most critical shortcoming found in much of the Bible teaching in my country is that *the Word is not practically applied to people's lives*. Bible truth is presented as abstract concepts, with no implications for how those truths can and should transform people's lives.

These shortcomings have consequences for the Christian community in Bangladesh. Churches limp along, barely surviving as they endure without spiritual vitality or vision for ministry. Believers drop out of church altogether, tired of the meager spiritual diet. And unbelievers are not attracted to the gospel when scriptural truth is presented to them in a dull, academic fashion.

In my ministry, InterVarsity Christian Fellowship of Bangladesh, we actually face criticism when we succeed in making the Scriptures compelling and meaningful for our students. When we attract young people through inductive Bible study that seeks to bring God's Word to life, we are accused of stealing young people away from the church. But we deliberately do not program on Sundays so as not to compete with local churches. We frequently encourage our students to attend local churches in their area. But despite our entreaties, many of our young people avoid the church–because nothing there speaks to them.

DRY ROOTS: THE CULTURAL CONTEXTS

THERE ARE REASONS why the Church in Bangladesh struggles to produce pastors and leaders who can bring the Bible to life. They are rooted in cultural patterns and traditions that are pervasive in Bangladesh society. Unfortunately, these patterns and traditions have also found a home in the Body of Christ:

Fixation on achievement. In Bangladeshi culture, high priority is placed on the attainment of recognizable achievements. In education, this translates into getting top marks on tests, successfully memorizing the content of textbooks, and writing papers that contain the information required by the professors. It does not necessarily include actually learning the subject. The drive for achievement is exacerbated by the educational system in Bangladesh, which emphasizes rote memorization and studying to the test over the acquisition of meaningful knowledge and practical skills.

This fixation on obtaining a graduation certificate rather than gaining mastery of the material can produce graduates with crippling limitations: engineers who cannot solve problems, IT workers who are overwhelmed by new software, and teachers who lack the ability to actually teach their students. It has also created a society that overly values such marks of achievement. Without the proper certificate, a person is automatically considered unfit for their position, regardless of their actual gifts and skills.

We find this same overemphasis on achievement in the Christian community. "My organization made me come to Bible school," a young man told me. He and I were fellow students at Bible school outside of the country. "Why did they make you attend?" I asked. "Even though I had a fruitful ministry, I don't have a Bible school certificate," he replied. "In their eyes, I'm not a 'real' minister. They told me if I did not get my certificate, I would not be promoted."

Bible school can even be seen as the school of last resort for parents desperate for their son or daughter to obtain a degree. "Our child did not score high enough on their exams to be admitted to the university or to the colleges," I have heard parents say. "[Such-and-Such] Bible school will admit our child–it is their last chance for a certificate." How will such graduates emerge with the heart and skills needed to effectively teach the Word of God?

Top-down teachers. Bangladeshi culture is rigidly hierarchical. Authority figures wield great power over those below them. In the educational system, this creates a huge gap between teachers and their students. As these teachers see it, their job is to come to class, download rote information to their students a one-way gusher, and leave. There is no need to actually get to know their students, listen to their perspectives, learn about their needs, or connect with them as people.

This hierarchy and rigidity is expressed in many ways, both big and small. For example, when a teacher enters the room, the students all stand. It is a gesture of respect. That is fair enough; but rather than simply sitting back down, they must remain standing until instructed by the teacher: "Okay, sit!" It is not a greeting–it is a command. (This protocol exists all of the way through university-level education.)

This same gulf between teacher and student exists in many of our Bible schools. The gap prevents students from doing anything but falling in with the rote, mechanical Bible instruction they are receiving from their teachers. Even more crippling, this top-down model prevents teachers from being able to teach from the example of their own lives. Their elevated position and rigidity of approach makes them unknowable to their students.

Education for the wrong reasons. One would hope that a person entering medical school does so, at least in part, with the goal of helping others. Unfortunately, in Bangladesh this is often not the case. A doctor enjoys great status and prestige in my country–along with the opportunity to become wealthy.

A path taken by many young people in Bangladesh pursuing prestige and wealth is as follows. First, try to get into medical school. If that fails, pursue engineering. If that fails, study something at the University of Dhaka or (if they cannot qualify for UD) a private university. They are pursuing vocation, but for the wrong reasons.

Similar corrupt motives can be found among those studying for the ministry. I still remember some of the goals shared with me by my fellow students at that out-of-country Bible school:

"If I get this certificate, I can get a good job."

"A Bible school education will make me attractive to prospective husbands."

"I want to get into a church or organization that will pay me a good salary."

Bible school graduates who pursue their degrees with these sorts of motives are poor candidates to become compelling teachers of the Scriptures.

Just-in-time culture. You might think the lack of preparation demonstrated by the Bible teacher I booked for our student conference was unusual. Unfortunately, this just-in-time approach is characteristic of our culture. We Bangladeshi too often believe that we can prepare for a task or endeavor with relatively little preparation.

I imagine you would presume that a national team representing its country in a major sport would prepare virtually full time. Not so in Bangladesh. Before a recent major competition, for example, the Bangladesh national cricket team began preparations just four weeks before their first match. (Not surprisingly, they did not enjoy success.)

Over-commitment. In our culture, it is very difficult to say no. To do so can be seen as insulting. In fact, the phrase we often use when indirectly trying to say no in the politest possible way is, "I will try."

Once someone completes school and enters into the ministry, this inability to say no can quickly breed over-commitment. Vital preparation time needed to create compelling sermons and Bible studies evaporates as one is asked to accept one extra commitment after another.

I have experienced the fallout that results from over-commitment, especially as I receive more and more requests to preach. Not only am I short-changing the time I need to adequately prepare for my primary teaching commitments, I have no time to prepare for the additional engagements I have accepted. Just-in-time kicks in as I present one off-the-cuff message after another.

This problem becomes more acute when one rises to a position of authority. My position as president of IVCF Bangladesh causes me to be besieged with invitations to preach and speak that are related to my position. I may be invited because the church or event organizers feel that someone with my title will provide added prestige. They may consider anyone with a title like mine to automatically be a better preacher or teacher. Or they may even invite me because they want to ask for favors from my organization. Whatever the motives, I am in a position where I have to juggle, and even sometimes refuse, more requests to preach and speak than I could ever fulfill.

TEACHING THE WORD
FROM SCRIPTURE'S PERSPECTIVE

SCRIPTURE ITSELF GIVES us a very different perspective on how God's truth should be taught. The purpose of teaching the Bible is not to pass along head knowledge, but to transform lives. And this transformational teaching was done in community–from generation to generation, life on life.

Even as God's Word was evolving in what we now know as Old Testament times, the Jewish community was instructed to remember what God had done for them and to pass along what they had seen and heard to future generations:

Watch yourselves closely so that you do not forget the things your eyes have seen or let them fade from your heart as long as you live. Teach them to your children and to their children after them. Remember the day you stood before the LORD your God at Horeb, when he said to me, "Assemble the people before me to hear my words so that they may learn to revere me as long as they live in the land and may teach them to their children."

Deuteronomy 4:9-10

It was the responsibility of the parents to teach their children, in both formal and informal ways: repeating God's Word when they were at home, when they were away, when they were working, and when they were resting. God's Word was to be applied to every aspect of life and human activity:

These commandments that I give you today are to be on your hearts. Impress them on your children. Talk about them when you sit at home and when you walk along the road, when you lie down and when you get up. Tie them as symbols on

*your hands and bind them on your foreheads. Write them
on the doorframes of your houses and on your gates.*

Deuteronomy 6:6-9

Transformational teaching implies that there will be meaningful outcomes when God's Word is taught and shared in compelling ways. While there are many such outcomes, two have particular importance for the teacher of Scripture.

Building moral and righteous character. In the lives of biblical heroes such as Joseph, Esther, and Daniel, we are given models for what it means to live righteously before God, even in the face of trials and persecution. We are taught that living as followers of Christ involves the development of moral and righteous character.

Jesus himself was a diligent student of the Scriptures (Luke 2:46-47). As a young boy, he was obedient and responsible to his earthly parents. As a spiritual leader and teacher, he was loving and kind, caring for the sick, the lepers, the children, the widows, and the poor. He demonstrated humility, even stooping to wash his disciples' feet (John 13:3-17). Even as the Son of God, he took on the form of a servant and was obedient unto death (Philippians 2:6-11).

The Bible also addresses down-home aspects of character. A just-in-time culture like mine should seriously ponder the words of Proverbs:

One who is slack in his work
is brother to one who destroys.

Proverbs 18:9

Sluggards do not plow in season;
so at harvest time they look but find nothing.

Proverbs 20:4

Calling the believer to action. The key to teaching truth that transforms is that *it has practical application.* Bible truth is not merely abstract, intellectual concepts. It is Spirit-inspired truth that calls us to respond.

Jesus' summary of the whole truth of the Scriptures is nothing but a call to action:

"'Love the Lord your God with all your heart and with
all your soul and with all your mind.' This is the first
and greatest commandment. And the second is like
it: 'Love your neighbor as yourself.' All the Law and
the Prophets hang on these two commandments."

Matthew 22:37-40

Do not merely listen to the word, and so
deceive yourselves. Do what it says.

James 1:22

Our teaching of Scripture should reflect this emphasis on applying the Bible's truths to our lives. This is one of the most crippling shortcomings in much of the Bible teaching done in my country.

SHIFTING THE PARADIGM: BIBLE TEACHING THAT TRANSFORMS

SO IS CHANGE POSSIBLE? Can Bangladesh begin to produce Bible teachers who can present compelling transformational truth from the Scriptures? I believe that such change is possible. But it will necessarily require us to shift key paradigms in our culture.

I was once asked, "If you were made president of a Bible school, how would you ensure that you produced graduates who were equipped to teach the Bible in a compelling way?" With humility, I believe the following steps would set this hypothetical school–and our country–on such a track:

Committed prayer. First, I would enter into a season of committed, consistent prayer. I would seek God to discern his best will for our school, our staff, and our students.

Listen to the students. Next, I would survey the students. My goal would be to discover who they are, find out what they need, and make it a priority to respond to the legitimate needs of the students, rather than demand that the students conform to a top-down hierarchy.

I would ask the question, "Why are you here?" in an effort to help students discern their motives. Where those motives were off-base, I would present them with an alternative: seeking after God's heart, pursuing a calling to ministry that will make an eternal difference in the lives of hundreds, perhaps thousands, of people who have yet to hear the Good News of the gospel.

Share the vision. Gathering my staff together, I would share with them our vision for the school–a school where the staff were committed to serving the students, rather than the other way around. Modeling the humility shown by Christ, we would seek to lead by example, letting students get to know us and opening our lives to them.

Leading by example would be manifested most powerfully when we would:

Close the gap between teacher and student. Rather than a model of teacher-as-guru, we would foster an environment where teachers served as friends and mentors to their students. Students would learn from the lives of their teachers as well as from their teaching in the classroom.

This closer, more nurturing relationship could be manifested in big and little ways. Remember my recounting of the protocol for a teacher entering a room? What if, after the students rise when the teacher enters the room, instead of a shouted command, the teacher would respond with, "Have a seat, please." Or even, "Good morning. How are you?" Does that sound like a little thing to you? In Bangladesh, it would be huge.

Perhaps the notion of teacher-as-mentor sounds fairly ordinary to you. But in the Bengali language, there is no word for mentor. While there are words that come close (such as "advisor"), the majority of Bangladeshi do not yet understand the concept of mentor.

This fact of language illustrates how large of a paradigm shift the introduction of teacher-as-mentor would be in our culture. But such a shift would be vital in developing graduates with the spiritual depth, practical skills, and emotional confidence to effectively teach the Scriptures.

Finally, and most importantly, the students in our Bible school would be trained to:

Emphasize the practical application of Scripture. The focus would be on how the truths found in the Bible can be applied to the everyday lives of people here and now. This emphasis on practical application is what brings the Bible to life. It would be the single most important element in changing Bible teaching from a dry, wooden exercise to a compelling, life-transforming experience.

CHANGING CULTURE...ONE STEP AT A TIME

IN SHARING MY DREAMS for this hypothetical Bible school, I harbor no illusions as to the challenges we would face. Cultural DNA is a powerful thing. It has inertia that has been built up over hundreds, even thousands, of years. And change of any kind is difficult for human beings. A pastor friend of mine has a great saying about the difficulty of change: "The only person who likes change is a wet baby. And the baby cries the whole time it is being changed."

But like the persistent widow (Luke 18:1-8), we can hold onto the hope that, as we pray and never give up, the Lord will honor our faith. We can envision a time when more and more men and women will emerge, burning with the heart of God and equipped to share and teach his holy Word in compelling, transforming, practical ways—ways that will touch the hearts, lives, and souls of both believers and those still searching for the Light.

And the things you have heard me say in the presence of many witnesses entrust to reliable people who will also be qualified to teach others.

2 Timothy 2:2

Lead Like Jesus

A Trans-Cultural Look at Christian Leadership

MENG AUN HOUR

In October 1991, Cambodia began to climb out of the nightmare years of the Khmer Rouge regime. This move to democracy created an opening for the gospel to come into Cambodia, with new freedom to preach and teach the Bible.

With this new freedom came foreigners–many as missionaries and leaders of Christian NGOs. We began an era of strong growth. From 1993 to 1997, the Church in Cambodia grew from 45 to 4,500 churches.

This growth bred confidence, especially amongst some of our foreign friends. They taught us that we could trust God in all situations–that God would protect us, provide for us, and free us from worry.

This teaching was hard to accept at first. We had just come through a period of mass slaughter and horror known as *The Killing Fields*, when millions of Cambodians were murdered for "disloyalty" to the Communist regime, for being educated, or simply for being in the wrong place at the wrong time. How should we reconcile our recent experience with this new, confident teaching?

We did our best to absorb the confidence that radiated from our foreign teachers–that is, until July 1997, when war broke out between rival political factions in the new, democratic Cambodia. We then watched in astonishment as our foreign friends fled–to Thailand, Malaysia, Singapore, and elsewhere. We Cambodian Christians were left to fend for ourselves.

This experience taught me that when it comes to understanding what it means to be a Christian leader, we should not look to fallible human beings. There is one Person to whom we should look–Jesus.

WHY WE NEED TO LEAD LIKE JESUS

"For my thoughts are not your thoughts,
neither are your ways my ways,"
declares the LORD.

"As the heavens are higher than the earth,
so are my ways higher than your ways
and my thoughts than your thoughts."

Isaiah 55:8-9

WE ARE IN AN ERA in which Christian leadership development is quite popular. There are many training programs and perspectives being presented. Many of these programs emphasize *contextualization*–that we apply cultural and other factors to our understanding of Christian leadership.

Cultural factors are real, and should be considered at the appropriate time. But before we do that, I suggest that we begin with a fundamental truth–that God's ways are not our ways. The leadership principles displayed by Jesus will often run counter to our human perspectives–*and they transcend cultures*. The leadership fundamentals expressed by Christ supercede particular cultural contexts. We must begin there before we move into contextual applications.

JESUS LEADERSHIP PRINCIPLE #1
ACTIONS SPEAK LOUDER THAN WORDS

His mother said to the servants, "Do whatever he tells you."

John 2:5

IN CAMBODIA, we have a saying: "Words alone do not cook rice." In the same way, Christian leadership is not about speaking, preaching, or teaching–it is about *living* what we teach or preach. This is the first principle Jesus teaches us about leadership–and it is a principle that transcends cultural contextualization.

We lived through the horror of how actions can speak louder than words in my country. The years of 1975 to 1979 were the time of the Pol Pot regime–*The Killing Fields*.

Khmer Rouge massacred millions of men, women, and children—all tied to an insane dream.

The goal was to identify all those in the population who were educated, had successful jobs, and held high-level positions in their communities, and then to kill them. Once all of the "wasteful elite" was eliminated, Cambodia would flourish as an agrarian utopia. But...how to identify those earmarked for destruction?

The Khmer Rouge adopted a diabolically ingenious method to uncover the "wasteful elite." They would arrive in a community with greetings of friendship. "We want to get to know you so that we can serve you better," they would say. Then, in the friendliest manner imaginable, they would begin to ask seemingly innocent questions: "What is your family's profession? Where were you educated? Who are the leaders in your community?"

At first, we were relieved by their gentleness and freely answered their questions. Then, as the educated and successful were led off to slaughter or murdered right in front of our eyes, we realized how the Khmer Rouge's actions countered their silky words.

That time of horror has left its mark. Today, Cambodians trust not at all in what is said to them. Compliments and kind words mean little. We have heard it all before, with deadly results. The only thing that matters to us is your *actions*.

You say that you love us with the love of Christ? Wonderful...but we will determine how true your words are by how you demonstrate your love through action. No other way.

Do not merely listen to the word, and so deceive yourselves. Do what it says.

James 1:22

JESUS LEADERSHIP PRINCIPLE #2
CONSISTENCY IS KEY

Jesus Christ is the same yesterday and today and forever.

Hebrews 13:8

AS CAMBODIA OPENED up to the gospel in the early 1990s, a school was established by foreign missionaries, designed to enable pastors and other leaders to obtain quality theological education that was affordable and accessible.

The missionary heading up this school encouraged us that the Church in Cambodia could raise up and serve God with national leaders. "As God used Moses to bring Israel out from Egypt, a widow to provide food to Elijah, and a young boy to provide food that ultimately fed 5,000 people," he told us, "God can use you in the Church in Cambodia to reach your country for Christ."

Then...in 2011, differences began to surface between foreign and national leaders as to how the school should move forward. At that point, we were told of a new policy:

"The executive director will not be Khmer. No Cambodians will hold leadership positions in the school–decision-making authority will be in the hands of foreigners. Otherwise, the school will be closed."

You can imagine how that felt to us. Most painfully, we felt the inconsistency between what they *said* about ministry partnership and how they *acted* when differences arose.

We learned a hard lesson through this experience. As Jesus lived out consistency in all aspects of his life, including as a leader, our actions *must* be consistent with our words if we are to have integrity as Christian leaders. Again, this is a *trans-cultural* truth.

As painful as this experience was, God used it to open my eyes. He is calling me, and us, to understand what it means to trust. First and foremost, we are to trust him in our lives. Does this mean we never trust other people? Not at all...but we need to be aware of human limitations and avoid putting trust in people rather than in Christ.

JESUS LEADERSHIP PRINCIPLE #3
KNOW HOW TO USE POWER

*That power is the same as the mighty strength he exerted
when he raised Christ from the dead and seated him at
his right hand in the heavenly realms, far above all rule
and authority, power and dominion, and every name
that is invoked, not only in the present age but also in the*

one to come. And God placed all things under his feet and appointed him to be head over everything for the church.

Ephesians 1:19b-22

This passage reminds us that Jesus, as God, has all power and authority. We all acknowledge this. The key to Jesus' power in the context of leadership is that *he knew how to effectively exercise that power.*

We all see many examples of how power can be exercised. But it is intriguing that throughout the Bible we see God the Father, Jesus, and the Holy Spirit exercising power primarily *to build relationships.*

Then the man and his wife heard the sound of the LORD God as he was walking in the garden in the cool of the day, and they hid from the LORD God among the trees of the garden. But the Lord God called to the man, "Where are you?"

Genesis 3:8-9

From the beginning of time, God's desire has been to be in relationship with his creation. Even at this early (and dark) point in the journey, God is walking the garden, looking for Adam and Eve, wanting to fellowship with them, even after their rebellion and sin. What is the creation, after all, but God exercising his power to create beings with whom he can relate–we humans?

The Word became flesh and made his dwelling among us. We have seen his glory, the glory of the one and only Son, who came from the Father, full of grace and truth.

John 1:14

God could have made himself known to us in any number of ways. But he chose to literally become flesh and dwell among humanity, the people he created for relationship. John 1 describes the progression–from Father to Son, to us, full of grace and truth.

Why did the Word choose to become flesh? Jesus did so to provide us with something, *someone*, with whom we could relate. Why dwell among us? So that Jesus can also, literally, relate with us.

Here I am! I stand at the door and knock; if anyone hears my voice and opens the door, I will come in and eat with that person, and they with me.

Revelation 3:20

In Asian cultures like Cambodia, there is no more important act of relationship than the sharing of food. It is the most fundamental expression of bonding and friendship. Conversely, to refuse to eat or share tea with another usually signals a break in the relationship. Jesus uses the example of eating with someone to emphasize his earnest desire to have deep fellowship with us. He is ready, if we are willing, to share the ultimate act of friendship in his culture.

Jesus' examples of how he used his power—to build relationships built not on law, but on love—can help us to understand how to use the power God grants us as Christian leaders.

In 2011, when the problems began at the theological school, I began spending a lot of time with God in his Word and in prayer. I asked him, "Lord, if you were in my place right now, how would you respond to these problems?"

God began to walk me through his Word. He showed me that, while he does have all authority, he does not use his authority to dominate or intimidate, but to build relationships with people. This is what Jesus did—with his disciples, with the crowds that followed him, and with the sick, crippled, and demon-possessed men and women who beseeched him for aid. Even from the beginning in Genesis, God walked and talked with Adam every day.

I became aware that the fundamental problem we faced at the school was that the use of power was being misunderstood and misapplied. Leaders, both foreign and Khmer, were using authority, power, and position to dominate and intimidate, rather than to build bridges of relationship.

John Alley, a man I consider my spiritual father, said that ministry is based on relationship, and relationship is the key to success. He told me, "Success is not about just reaching the goal or finishing the tasks. Ultimately, success is about the loving relationships we can build."

Relationship develops Unity.

Relationship builds Trust.

Relationship makes Teamwork possible.

JESUS LEADERSHIP PRINCIPLE #4
TO LEAD IS TO SERVE

In your relationships with one another,
have the same mindset as Christ Jesus:
Who, being in very nature God,
did not consider equality with God
something to be used to his own advantage;
rather, he made himself nothing
by taking the very nature of a servant,
being made in human likeness.
And being found in appearance as a man,
he humbled himself
by becoming obedient to death—
even death on a cross!

Philippians 2:5-8

WHEN FOREIGN MISSIONARIES and Christian NGO leaders first came to Cambodia, they arrived with a humble spirit. They wanted to spend time with local pastors and leaders and build good relationships.

But over time, as they got to know the language and became familiar with the culture, pride began to creep in.

Some of our friends began to spend less time with us and more time with one another.

When foreigners would meet one another for the first time, the question they always asked was, "How long have you been in Cambodia?" The longer one lived here, the more value and honor one felt. This sense of place increased if the missionary or NGO leader married a Cambodian.

In this competition to be the most acclimatized foreigner in Cambodia, our friends lost sight of the big picture–the Cambodian pastors and leaders who were born in Cambodia, have lived their whole lives here, and were serving God long before missionaries came to our country. Sadly, many of our friends forgot a fundamental tenet of leading like Jesus: *to lead is to serve.*

The relationships Jesus built were not transactional relationships, developed just to serve a purpose. Jesus longs to be with us until the end of the earth–forever and ever. In the same way, we are to build relationships that serve others, relationships that will last for this life and beyond.

Slowly, I am learning how to apply the leadership principles of Jesus to my own ministry. Recently, a 12-year veteran of my church staff came to me. He told me that he wanted to stop working with our church to take a position with a Christian NGO.

Years ago, my encounter with this man would have been brief. I would have taken his desire to leave as disloyalty, given him his leave, and never spoken with him again.

But I have learned that the relationships of love that Jesus wants us to develop mean that we are committed to those relationships for the long term.

I have invested much time with this young leader. We have met several times and continue to meet regularly as I try my best to understand why he wants to make this change. Beyond mere understanding, I want him to know that I am care for him and love him as a person, whether he stays or leaves. I want this young man to understand that our relationship will continue, even if we no longer work in the same organization.

JESUS LEADERSHIP PRINCIPLE #5
LEADING LIKE JESUS MEANS FREEDOM

WE HUMANS ARE PRONE to compare ourselves to one another. When we fall into this trap, we usually head down one of two dead-end roads: *pride* or *discouragement*. As happened with some of my foreign friends, they began to see themselves as better than us (Cambodians). And as we compared ourselves to them, we became discouraged by our lack of education, expertise, and resources.

The beauty of leading like Jesus is that we are released from the prison of pride and discouragement. As we...

- let our actions speak louder than our words

- make our deeds consistent with our words

- use our power to build caring, long-term relationships

- lead to serve others

...we are free to be the Christ-honoring, kingdom-building leaders that God created us to be. And these leadership principles given to us by Jesus are true for all of us, no matter what our backgrounds, ethnicities, or cultures.

What is my leadership style?

Am I leading like Jesus?

Redeeming the Already There

Developing the Leader God has Already Created

TAKESHI TAKAZAWA

"No, I don't want to become a Christian."
I was stunned. My friend and I had just finished debating the existence of God and the resurrection of Jesus. I had given sound arguments to prove the existence of God and that his Son Jesus rose from the dead. My friend even admitted to the logic of my conclusions. But he had no interest in becoming a Christ follower.

"You admit that I'm right, but you refuse to accept Christ," I said. "Why do you say no?" "Because," he answered, "I do not want to become like you."

LEGACY OF THE INCOMPLETE

I SHARE THIS DISCOURAGING story from my past only to make a point. It highlights the paradigm from which, at that time, I understood God to view humanity: *People are lost.*

As Christians, we know this to be true. Scripture makes it clear that, without God, we are without hope:

> *Remember that at that time you were separate from Christ,*
> *excluded from citizenship in Israel and foreigners to the cove-*
> *nants of the promise, without hope and without God in the world.*

Ephesians 2:12

Understanding our lost state is a foundational component to understanding our human identity in the eyes of God. But it is not the only component. Scripture also tells us that, from the very beginning, we have had within us the image and likeness of God–and that it is good:

> *Then God said, "Let us make mankind in our image, in our*
> *likeness"...So God created mankind in his own image, in the*
> *image of God he created them; male and female he created*
> *them....God saw all that he had made, and it was very good.*

Genesis 1:26a, 27, 31

How we view the human condition deeply affects how we treat people. If we solely see people as lost, as missing, then we will only see them as hopeless, worthless objects that need to be found. However, if we see people as both lost and made in the image of God, then we will treat them differently. We will see them as valuable creations whom God wants to bring back to where they belong. God is not trying to add something to a person's life that they don't already have; rather, he seeks to buy them back to himself and bring them back to the life for which they were originally created–to live in fellowship with God himself.

But as a Japanese man who became a Christian almost forty years ago, I have learned that this understanding is not widely shared. The Christianity that has been taught here in Japan reflects a dramatically different understanding of the human condition. It sees people as utterly and only lost. This perspective, while not overtly taught, was embedded in the presuppositions brought by Western missionaries. It permeated our thinking and practice: P*eople who do not know Christ are lost. Their cultures are pagan and evil. They need to be saved and educated, step by step, in proper doctrine so that they will eventually be able to follow Christ on their own.*

This thinking is not just a fact from the past. It continues in many places in Japan, and other parts of the world, even today. The implications this has had, and continues to have, on outreach, discipleship, and leader development in my country have been profound. Unfortunately, most of the implications have been negative.

THIRD WAY TO WHOLENESS

THE INTENT OF THIS chapter is not to cast blame or to set up a debate between lostness versus dormancy. My hope is that as we better understand a more holistic picture of how God has created and views us, we can begin together a journey to wholeness in Christ.

It is a lifelong journey that we all share. My hope is that in sharing a little bit of my journey, we will be encouraged and, together, continue to grow in our understanding of who we are and who we can become in the sight of God.

It is like the blind man who was healed by Jesus in successive steps:

> *They came to Bethsaida, and some people brought a blind man and begged Jesus to touch him. He took the blind man by the hand and led him outside the village. When he had spit on the man's eyes and put his hands on him, Jesus asked, "Do you see anything?"*
>
> *He looked up and said, "I see people; they look like trees walking around."*
>
> *Once more Jesus put his hands on the man's eyes. Then his eyes were opened, his sight was restored, and he saw everything clearly.*
>
> *Mark 8:23-25*

Many of us are like that blind man after the first application of spit. Our incomplete understanding of God's view of us causes us to see, but blurrily. The people look like trees. We need further touches from Jesus to grasp the whole truth of how we can live and develop as God intends.

We must grow in holistic and complete understanding of the human condition. Otherwise, what we do can be quite different from what God calls us to do. Our view needs to be enlarged. That is why the process of Jesus clearing our vision is so crucial–and is a lifelong process that we all share in our journey of faith.

This chapter highlights three areas where this incomplete understanding–this blurry vision–has had impact in my country: evangelism, discipleship, and leader development. And we will also look at how God has helped me so far to gain a clearer vision of holistic, integrated approaches in these same areas. I hope that sharing my journey can encourage you.

WINNING THE ARGUMENT—LOSING THE SOUL

I BECAME A CHRISTIAN through an English class offered by a church plant seeking to attract Japanese interested in learning the language. Converted as a young boy, I was one of the "first fruits" of this church plant. I began to absorb the perspectives and values of the ministry that had reached me.

In most ministry throughout Japan, evangelism was understood as engaging in cognitive explanation. The idea was that once people understood the gospel in their minds, they would naturally accept Christ. Once they understood that they were lost, they would want to be found.

So as a young Christian, I began to share my new faith. I attended Bible school at night to become better equipped as a Christian. At Bible school, I was introduced to apologetics.

This apologetic knowledge was taught as the secret to leading people to Christ. How easy it would be once they understood the truth of God! But like the above encounter with my friend, being exposed to the "rightness" of my information did not create in people a desire to respond. In fact, it created the opposite.

What I came to realize over time (and with the help of a lot of negative feedback) was that this intellectually based, confrontational approach was felt by most Japanese to be foreign and, quite frankly, American. It grated against Japanese sensibilities, such as the value of maintaining harmony and not engaging in personal debate.

But in my thinking, these people were lost, so nothing they said, or had, was valid. They did not have what I had–and I needed to give it to them. I did not then see that my friend, like everyone, was made in Christ's image. God was already working in his life to bring my friend back to himself. God was working to bring what was dormant in my friend back to life.

FROM LECTURER TO LISTENER

THEN, GOD STARTED the process of beginning to clear my vision to help me see God's redemptive perspective, through looking at how Jesus engaged in evangelism. As I examined the Scriptures, it dawned on me that Jesus never did sales talks. While he often defended himself against accusations brought by hostile detractors, he wasn't about winning debates. Rather, Jesus' approach to outreach was to become human, specifically a Jewish man:

In your relationships with one another,
have the same mindset as Christ Jesus:
Who, being in very nature God,

did not consider equality with God
something to be used to his own advantage;
rather, he made himself nothing
by taking the very nature of a servant,
being made in human likeness.

And being found in appearance as a man,
he humbled himself
by becoming obedient to death–
even death on a cross!

Philippians 2:5-8

Jesus ate with sinners. He spoke with women who were considered outcasts. He used language, culture, and his very humanness to reach people. For Jesus, evangelism wasn't about words–it was about his life.

In the same way, the apostle Paul's priority was to incarnate for the sake of reaching others:

Though I am free and belong to no one, I have made myself
a slave to everyone, to win as many as possible. To the Jews
I became like a Jew, to win the Jews. To those under the law
I became like one under the law (though I myself am not
under the law), so as to win those under the law. To those
not having the law I became like one not having the law
(though I am not free from God's law but am under Christ's
law), so as to win those not having the law. To the weak I

became weak, to win the weak. I have become all things to all people so that by all possible means I might save some.

1 Corinthians 9:19-22

Evangelism was not about winning arguments; it was about connecting with people. It wasn't about honing the proper technique, or perfecting the ideal sales pitch. Evangelism was about allowing the Holy Spirit to work through me to bring someone—someone who was lost *and* made in God's image—back into the divine relationship for which that person was always created.

Now, when I interact with someone, I try to focus more on asking questions. I attempt to get to know the person, listen to their thoughts, and seek to understand their situation, their problems. I pray that God will help me be his agent of redemption as Jesus restores what is damaged and nurtures what is dormant, rather than me just shoving the right information onto the person. I try my best to not get caught up in the *hows*—I attempt to focus on seeing how the Holy Spirit is going to breathe life into the person, to redeem the already there.

DISCIPLESHIP? BRING OUT THE MANUAL

WHEN I FIRST BECAME a Christian, it was explained to me that I needed to grow as a disciple in the Lord. I really thought "discipleship" meant joining a class that methodically worked through a textbook. As a new believer, I was ready to dive in. I signed up for the course—a series of systematic activities that resulted in a mechanistic understanding of discipleship.

Bible study was equally systematic. Small groups pursued curricula designed to impart head knowledge in a linear stream. We followed templates for what was called discipleship through which life was expected to conform.

The challenge was, life did not always conform to those templates. It seems like there were major disconnects between what we studied and the messy realities in the lives of many people in the group.

Regularly, we would be shocked to discover brothers and sisters who had developed relationships with nonbelievers whom they intended to marry, or who continued with unhealthy habits. These realities damaged the spiritual development and very spiritual lives of these brothers and sisters.

But did these life realities distract us from the systematic plan? Not at all! Ignoring the situations before us, we would plunge ahead as instructed with the next chapter in our discipleship textbook. All the while, our struggling brothers and sisters would eventually fall away as the disconnects would become too great. "That is so unfortunate," we would say. "Brother So-and-So has backslidden." Or, "Sister So-and-So must not be a real Christian." Or, "It turns out that Brother So-and-So is lost."

Over time, God led me to realize that my understanding of discipleship may not be what God intended to begin with. I needed a different perspective.

JESUS' DISCIPLESHIP "TEMPLATE": LIFE ON LIFE

AGAIN I WAS DRAWN to look at the life of Jesus. What did discipleship look like in his life? I began to notice that he called people to follow him. Discipleship happened as they walked the journey together:

> As Jesus was walking beside the Sea of Galilee, he saw two brothers, Simon called Peter and his brother Andrew. They were casting a net into the lake, for they were fishermen. "Come, follow me," Jesus said, "and I will send you out to fish for people." At once they left their nets and followed him.
>
> Going on from there, he saw two other brothers, James son of Zebedee and his brother John. They were in a boat with their father Zebedee, preparing their nets. Jesus called them, and immediately they left the boat and their father and followed him.
>
> Matthew 4:18-22

Jesus did not pursue a systematic curriculum. He taught his disciples out of the issues that arose as they journeyed. He met people at their starting points–whether it be the fishermen, the tax collector, the woman at the well, or the centurion–and from there, led them toward the Father.

Discipleship from Jesus' perspective was life-on-life, engaging real people grappling with real problems and providing real solutions from the One with the power to solve. It was unsystematic, messy, and transforming.

SET DOWN THE TEMPLATE, PICK UP THE PERSON

SIMILARLY TO THE SHIFT in my understanding of evangelism, my paradigm began to change in regard to discipleship as well. Before, I wholeheartedly believed that getting insight and knowledge was everything there was to being a good disciple. So I not only studied and followed the sequential curriculum, but I also encouraged others to do the same.

Now, discipleship became a focus on the person rather than on a program. I am learning to listen to and follow God together with fellow disciples on this journey of faith. *Where is this person in their journey? How might God want to restore, heal, and enhance this person? How does the living God want our relationship to be used to transform us? How might God want to speak his truth, wisdom, and love directly into the messiness of our lives?*

The beauty of life-on-life discipleship is that it takes us directly to the person of God. We go straight to our Creator, who uses the real issues of our lives to renew us through his Spirit. We are not following a template disconnected from real life: we are following him in the midst of the journey.

LEADER DEVELOPMENT:
THE *LITTLE HOUSE ON THE PRARIE* PROBLEM

WHEN I WAS APPOINTED to be the leader of a small congregation, I began to focus on executing all my "great" ideas for the church, including methods of creative evangelism as well as a strategy to increase the spiritual lives of the members. I also worked to capture, communicate, and cast the vision that God had given this church. I was so busy doing everything that I could. At the time I did not realize it, but looking back, I can see how this idea of church leadership spread here in Japan.

After World War II, there was a huge outpouring of Christian mission and ministry effort into Japan. Thousands of Christians from the West came to evangelize, disciple, and plant churches. They came with soft hearts and strong spirits–but they also largely came with the *utterly and only lost* view of humanity as their paradigm. Their predisposition was to reject the structures and practices they found in Japanese culture (which was, of course, lost) and replace it with "Christian" structures and practices–which meant, at the time, Western structures and practices.

This had major ramifications on leader development. Japanese people live, work, and lead in community. In order to sustain community over hundreds of years, Japanese society has developed overlapping layers, or generational groups, of leaders. These multi-generational layers empowered strong leadership development structures. For example, Japan has for centuries emphasized apprenticeship as a means to learn and develop skills. Whether they be mechanical, craft, or leadership skills, the principle has been, "Walk with me. Watch me. Learn. Do it together. And then help others do."

Unfortunately, the postwar church-planting model brought from the West was hierarchical, led by an all-powerful pastor. The church, rather than being an organic movement designed to reach people, was an institution to be managed by the pastor. The pastor was the absolute leader. The pastor set the agenda, mapped out the rules. Pastors did not develop teammates, but attracted followers. And they were expected to do everything themselves. They were in charge–and they were alone.

Looking back on my time of church leadership, I can see that this was my experience. I was trying to lead in an individualistic worldview manner in the context of a group culture. But since I saw that this group culture was Japanese and therefore lost, I stuck with the way I had been shown. I had expectations of being a good leader, but I wasn't as effective as I had hoped to be. Quite honestly, out of frustration that I could not execute it all, I lost motivation in regard to bringing "revolution" to this church.

There is an additional historical dynamic in our context. In the mid-1970s, the US television program *Little House on the Prairie* began to air in Japan. It was very popular and was watched and loved by millions. The irony was, the church of 1870 that was portrayed in the television program accurately depicted the type of church that had in fact been planted throughout Japan in the 1950s. This church model, with all good intentions, placed missionaries in charge as they attempted to rescue utterly lost people from an utterly lost culture. The concept of indigenous leadership development was not on the radar.

Leadership meant a single individual who, within the given authority and responsibility, did everything for the good of those served. In this paradigm, my leadership becomes about what I can accomplish with my ideas, styles, and authority during the period of time between when I started and ended as leader. Leader development was basically seen as leader replacement. This individualistic leadership style was very foreign to the community-based leadership style of my country, which sees leadership as moving in and with a community from one place to another over spans of leaders' lifetimes.

EQUIPPING THE SAINTS IS PLURAL

BUT THERE IS another paradigm for leadership develop-ment–God's. Let's again look at the life of Jesus as well as the ministry of Paul.

What is one of the first things Jesus did as he began his public ministry? He called and gathered his disciples. From then on, he invested in them as they journeyed together. With every incident, every miracle, every lesson–and every time the disciples got it wrong–Jesus was building into them, knowing that soon they would be the core leaders of his Church and his kingdom on earth.

Jesus also sent out and spent time with his followers in pairs or larger groups. Paul also was always traveling and ministering with others. And in the book of Ephesians, Paul describes a collective, collaborative model where the body of Christ is equipped to work together:

So Christ himself gave the apostles, the prophets, the evangelists, the pastors and teachers, to equip his people for works of service, so that the body of Christ may be built up until we all reach unity in the faith and in the knowledge of the Son of God and become mature, attaining to the whole measure of the fullness of Christ.

Ephesians 4:11-13

LEADERSHIP: A SHARED EXPERIENCE

WHILE GOD DEVELOPS distinctive roles, leadership in the Body of Christ is to be a shared experience. When Peter stood up to address the crowd at Pentecost, it says that he stood up "with the Eleven" (Acts 2:14). The Council of Jerusalem, writing the church in Antioch to address a thorny faith and practice issue, says, "It seemed good to the Holy Spirit and to us" (Acts 15:28). They decided together that Judas and Silas should accompany Paul and Barnabas to Antioch with the letter. In all these instances, believers functioned as a leadership community.

That is why we emphasize the model of *leadership community* throughout Asian Access. However well or poorly we may achieve it, our goal is to bring pastors together in learning communities, creating an environment where, over time, they can begin to get to know and trust one another deeply.

As their relationships develop, they can envision a future where leadership and responsibility can be shared, emerging leaders can be mentored rather than marginalized, and collaborative ministry can be launched for the advancement of the gospel in their churches, communities, and countries.

Wherever our place of service–whether it be as a local church pastor, a lay leader, or a believer called to make a difference in their workplace or community–the holistic understanding of who we are in God's eyes frees us to see ourselves and others as God intended. This more complete picture of humankind, that incorporates perspectives from different parts of the world, enables us to invest with passion in the development of all of God's people, especially our leaders.

LOST AND FOUND...AT THE SAME TIME

WE HUMANS ARE LOST. We are in utter need of God. It is by his power and Spirit that we are revived, restored, and renewed. But that is only part of the whole story. Even at the beginning of time, as God first created humankind, he made us in his image and likeness (Genesis 1:26). That image and likeness of God is in all of us–dormant, if we have not yet reached out to reconnect with our Creator–but it is there nonetheless.

Like the blind man in Mark 8, the healing of our vision by Jesus is not a one-time event. It is part of our lifelong journey as Christ followers. We are all on the path from blindness to clear sight together. It is an ongoing process, one which we will not complete in our earthly lifetime. We will mistake people for trees all along the way. But as we embrace the process, with God and with one another, the Spirit gives us hope that, when we do reach our eternal home, we will enjoy the clear sight that God always intended for his creation–formerly lost but now found, formerly dormant but now redeemed.

Dark Is Beautiful

Promoting God's People Values in a Skin-Deep World

KAVITHA EMMANUEL

Several years ago, I ran into a friend of mine as I was dropping my five-year-old daughter at school. A mother of two girls near my daughter's age, I knew her well. After we dropped our girls off, we decided to go for coffee and a chat.

We began talking about our children. As the conversation continued, she began to share about a developing situation with her two daughters. Her older daughter was getting a lot of positive attention. She was liked in school. Adults would hold her cheeks (an Indian way of showing affection). She was constantly being told how beautiful she was by passers-by.

The younger daughter, on the other hand, received no such attention. Her mother recounted a recent incident when they had visited a toy shop. Upon entering, the proprietor welcomed her older daughter with a balloon and candy, while ignoring the younger girl.

This mother ached in her heart for her younger girl. She did everything she could to affirm to her of her value and worth. But this little girl was only too aware of how she was viewed and treated. Just that week, the little girl had returned home from school and tearfully asked her mother, "Mom, I am so dark. That is why I am not beautiful, why I am not chosen for school photographs, why adults ignore me.

"Why am I so dark? And why is Sis so light?"

IF YOU'RE FAIR, YOU'RE GOLDEN—IF YOU'RE DARK...

INDIA IS A LAND OF a billion shades of skin–from chocolate hues, sun-kissed versions of beige, and golden-honey tints of brown to different shades of cream. But within this myriad of skin-tone variety, one value holds true: fair skin is beautiful, while dark skin is not. If you are born fair, you are fortunate...if you are born dark, you are not.

Skin-color bias thrives in India. It is virtually built into our cultural DNA. Without any sort of conscious realization, skin-color bias wreaks havoc on the sense of value and worth of millions of girls and boys, women and men.

Conversation about skin color is no secret in most Indian families. Common phrases we hear while growing up include:

- "Don't go out in the sun, you will get dark."

- "Use turmeric, save your color."

- "Use saffron in your milk to ensure your baby is born with fair skin."

- "Don't go swimming. It makes you tan."

When a child is born, there are two things people are interested in. First, is the child a boy? Second, how fair is the baby? A girl baby with dark skin is born with two strikes against her. Parents hear comments like, "Who will marry her?" "We need to save up for her dowry." *Dowry* is the practice of paying huge sums of money and/or valuables as a "bride price," given by the parents of the bride to the parents of the groom. Dowry is legally banned, but still commonly practiced in India.

Dowry drives many families into crushing debt. It contributes to evils like bride burning, divorce, and gendercide. And there are many stories of parents having to pay double-portion dowry for dark-skinned daughters. (You can learn more about the issue of dowry in my husband Jeyakaran's chapter, "The Powerhouse Journey," p. 203.)

I grew up in a family of very many different skin shades. My dad is dark-skinned and my mom is on the lighter side. I am on the lighter side as well. Because of this, I did not experience skin-color discrimination. I grew up oblivious to the damage it was doing to others. Like everyone, I too believed that to be fair meant to be beautiful.

GROWING IN FAITH—AND AWARENESS

MY ENCOUNTER WITH Christ happened early in life. I grew up in an authentic Christian home where we not only believed and professed our faith, but lived out what we believed. My parents have been my role models in embracing a lifestyle that demonstrates generosity, hospitality, kindness, and Christ-like leadership.

I can't remember a single day when we did not have non-family guests sharing our meals with us. My dad has always been known for his extravagance when it comes to giving to people–not because we had much (we didn't!), but because it gives him great joy to give. And the opportunities to give were all around us. We lived in a small town where many people suffered from poverty. There were starving and homeless people everywhere we went. This poverty was exacerbated by India's caste system, which teaches that all people are created unequal.

My parents both being teachers, we were a family that valued education, music, and the arts. We were expected to do well in school and pursue higher education. My parents saw teaching as mission. Into that mission, they built values that were actually counter to prevailing Indian culture. They laid the foundation in my heart that everyone was in fact created *equal.*

In many ways, we were an offbeat Indian family. In a culture where women are repressed, my mother was and is a leader–strong, confident, intelligent, and bold. My mother and father demonstrated equality in their marriage relationship in many ways, which was pretty radical in those days. This was all in stark contrast to what I saw around me. In our community, women were not treated as equals. To take up a job, a married woman needed her husband's and her in-laws' approval. I watched as men drank up their paychecks, beat their wives and kids, and had affairs with other women, while their wives lived in submission, viewing their suffering as their fate.

This often infuriated me. But what could I do? I was just a child who didn't understand the ways of the world. The message my community was sending me was that being a woman is a handicap. But my family experience taught me that this was not the truth.

Now my mother is no feminist. And my family, even though we are Christians, were to some degree influenced by gender, skin-color, and caste discrimination. We were caught in the toxic cycles of our culture. But through our faith, God empowered us to take at least some steps towards equality–steps that, at the time, were quite radical.

THE BIGGEST HURDLE: FEAR

WHAT MY UPBRINGING and life experience were teaching me was that one of the biggest hurdles we women have to overcome is *fear*. From birth, we are told that we are weak and are best off if we stay within the boundaries set for us. If we try to push past those boundaries, then we are not "good" women.

All my life, I had heard statements like: "A girl should be seen and not heard"; "Girls should be submissive"; Girls shouldn't go out too much"; "Boys are better than girls." But instead of submitting, I began to question and rebel against these norms. Whenever someone said I could not do something, it motivated me to prove them wrong.

I lived with my share of fear. I questioned God: "Why did you create women unequal? If I have to live my life like other women, what difference am I going to make? Lord, I want to be different." I struggled with the Scriptures that people cite to prove women are unequal. I wept and cried before God: "Lord, I want to serve you as well as any man." My understanding was that if I went to Bible college to study theology, my only option was to be a pastor's wife–not a role I desired.

THE MESSAGE FROM SCRIPTURE

AT THAT TIME, I didn't have anyone to whom I could turn to discuss or share my struggles. My questions seemed too out of bounds. But thankfully, instead of running away from God, I always ran to him with my questions. I was convinced that God's view of me, and of all women, was different from the accepted dogma of the time.

In desperation, I dove into the Bible to discern just what God did think of me. To my relief, I found that the arc of Scripture *affirmed* my equality before God.

I was reminded that God knew me before he formed me in my mother's womb:

> *For you created my inmost being;*
> *you knit me together in my mother's womb.*
> *I praise you because I am fearfully and wonderfully made;*

> *your works are wonderful,*
> *I know that full well.*
> *My frame was not hidden from you*
> *when I was made in the secret place,*
> *when I was woven together in the depths of the earth.*
> *Your eyes saw my unformed body;*
> *all the days ordained for me were written in your book*
> *before one of them came to be.*
>
> *Psalm 139:13-16*

I read that in Jesus' eyes, all humanity is equal, together, literally One:

> *So in Christ Jesus you are all children of God through faith,*
> *for all of you who were baptized into Christ have clothed*
> *yourselves with Christ. There is neither Jew nor Gentile,*
> *neither slave nor free, nor is there male and female, for you*
> *are all one in Christ Jesus. If you belong to Christ, then you*
> *are Abraham's seed, and heirs according to the promise.*
>
> *Galatians 3:26-29*

I was touched by the ways Jesus responded to women: his conversation with the Samaritan woman (John 4:7-26), his rescue of the condemned adulteress (John 8:1-11), his healing of the bleeding woman (Mark 5:21-43), and his sensitivity with Mary when confronted by Martha (Luke 10:38-42). I took courage from the lives of Abigail, Deborah, Esther, Miriam, Rahab, and even Eve. (Too often, we look only at Eve's fall, forgetting how God restored her. Within the consequences she had to face was the promise that God would crush the head of Satan through her offspring.)

To understand our value and worth as human beings, regardless of our gender, all we have to do is go to where it all started–to Eden:

> *God created man in his own image, in the image of God*
> *he created him; male and female he created them.*
>
> Genesis 1:27

> *He created them male and female and blessed them. And*
> *he named them "Mankind" when they were created.*
>
> Genesis 5:2

BRINGING THE WHOLE GOSPEL TO WOMEN

IN MY TEENAGE YEARS, I grew to realize that my life's mission was to bring the whole gospel to women who shared my struggles. I was convinced God had called me to be a woman who would stand in the gap for other women.

My confidence in who I was and in God's call for me grew as I stepped out of my comfort zone and started to talk to women about their God-given value, dignity, and worth. In my high school and college years, I led youth gatherings and women's groups, even while God was still working in me to help me know who I am. I found great satisfaction in letting women know how special they were. I spent hours talking to women about their dreams and their true potential, and encouraged them to go for their dreams in spite of stereotypical expectations from friends, family, society, and the church. I began to function as a worship leader, teacher, and leader in whatever capacities I could.

A CASTE-BREAKING MARRIAGE...OF EQUALS

AFTER I FINISHED school and began to think about my future, I concluded that if marriage was part of God's plan for my life, it would not limit my freedom in Christ in terms of what I did or who I believed I was. God was helping me to better understand his overriding value of mutual submission in marriage, as each partner seeks to serve and support the other.

When I was 25, I met Jeyakaran. He was a man after God's own heart, keen to challenge traditions that bound people in legalistic and religious chains. He had had his own journey of knowing Christ in a way that gave him a vision for the freedom that is found only in the gospel.

This journey led Jakes to make a vow: he would marry a woman from outside of his own caste, the notoriously conservative Nadars. He realized that his family and cultural tradition worked against Jesus' message of the full value of every human being, and he made a conscious decision to break away from this.

I do not belong to the same caste as Jakes. God in his sovereignty brought Jakes and me together. But caste freedom was one thing: the equality of men and women was another. It took a long time of prayer, study, and discussion for Jakes to see that God views and values men and women equally. It took more time and study for Jakes to affirm that God's call to service is based on gifting rather than gender. But he did–and we realized that God's calling on our lives would include spreading the news of God's full value and empowerment of everyone in his creation.

We began our journey together as leaders of Powerhouse, a church Jakes pioneered in 1997. It was a big learning curve for both of us at that time. We were just getting used to being married while at the same time figuring out the nuances of leading a church. It was a life of faith in all aspects–financially, relationally, and treading unknown paths in ministry. Every day, we had to fully rely on God's guidance, providence, and enablement. Gradually, God began to bless our efforts. Unchurched and churched people who were tired of ritualistic Christianity found Powerhouse a comfortable, affirming environment.

At Powerhouse, women served in all capacities, including worship leading, teaching, preaching, and pastoral care. It has been my joy to see women set free from fear and legalism embracing the gospel in all its wholeness. Our Powerhouse leadership team, comprised of both men and women (with more women than men actually committed to the mission of the church), was vital as we grew into a five-church network that ministered across metro Chennai.

WOMEN OF WORTH IS BORN

AFTER SEVERAL YEARS of ministry and study, I felt God's call to launch a women's ministry in Powerhouse to deepen and expand the empowerment of women in our church. We developed workshops, training, and support groups that helped the women at Powerhouse discover their gift-edness and strategize how to put their gifts into practice. Others began to hear about our work. We were asked to bring our teaching and workshops to other churches, associations, and denominations.

Women began to tell their unchurched friends about our message. Many of these women were their co-workers in the marketplace. "We face the same issues of devaluation and discrimination," they told us. "Can you help us?"

In 2003, Women of Worth became an official nonprofit program. WOW developed a two-pronged emphasis–to reach out to women in the world as well as women in the church. We organized conferences and workshops that addressed the needs of women in metro Chennai in all of their life contexts. Over the years, God not only used WOW to reach out to women in our own city, but he has helped us be a voice for women in national and global contexts.

In brief, WOW's vision is to empower women across cultures and ethnicities to stand up for *justice*, *equality*, and *change* in all facets of life and society, in both local and global contexts.

WOW seeks to empower women to:

- *Celebrate* who they are based on their innate value and unique potential
- *Anticipate* and give expression to the changes still needed for women
- *Participate* in social action that will continue to empower women

We are a small entity whom God has enabled to be big in influence. From our beginnings as an inwardly focused women's group, WOW now is known as one of the strong voices in India, championing women's human rights on varied platforms–from student campuses and national conferences to popular media.

THE ELEPHANT IN THE ROOM EMERGES

AS WOW CONDUCTED counselling sessions, workshops, and conferences for and with young women and children, one particular issue kept surfacing–skin color. Women and girls repeatedly pointed to the darkness of their skin as the main reason they felt less confident or less valuable. They considered themselves ugly and unattractive to prospective grooms. In some cases, these girls found it hard to find a groom.

In India, arranged and brokered marriage is still a prevalent tradition. We also still have a thriving print newspaper industry. If you were to browse through the classifieds, you would find a large matrimonial section. Here, parents advertise to find suitable grooms and brides. A few sample advertisements from a leading newspaper will give you an idea of what is being sought by these parents (bold emphasis mine):

> *Family seeks alliance for their well-educated, well-placed, tall, handsome son, 26 years, clean habits. Slim, **fair** and beautiful girls, MBA or CA preferred.*

> *TAMIL MUSLIM 27/172/MEd/PhD/Fair Rich Haji Family seek very **Fair** Bride*

> ***Fair** Well Settled Doctor Family Seeks Girl Same Caste pref. Medical Profession*

Marriage is *the* defining dynamic in Indian culture–as my husband Jakes mentions in his chapter, it is where "the rubber meets the road." In India, marriage match-making revolves around two criteria: caste and skin color. As you can see in the above advertisements, fair skin is a front-and-center requirement for a desirable mate.

A few years ago, one of our WOW team members was approached by a London-based Indian family for a marriage proposal. The groom was a doctor who had lost his legs in a road accident. My highly accomplished, talented, and beautiful friend was willing to overlook his physical limitations. "What matters to me most is a person's character," she said. "I am willing to consider this proposal."

The groom's parents came to visit my friend, then returned to London. For more than two months, my friend heard nothing. When she finally called to enquire what had happened, she was told she was too dark for their son. We couldn't digest what we heard. A wheelchair-bound man, burdened with the crippling limitations imposed upon him by a devastating accident, found my friend too dark to be his wife!

COLORISM DEFINED

SKIN-COLOR BIAS, or *colorism*, can be defined as prejudice or discrimination against individuals with a dark skin tone, typically among people of the same ethnic or racial group. In India, colorism is expressed openly–from marriage proposals to the multi-billion-dollar skin-whitening products industry. Globally, this toxic perspective corrodes the self-worth of countless individuals, men as well as women.

In India, the preference for fair skin is not even considered a discriminatory practice. As I've mentioned, cosmetic companies make billions through their lines of skin-whitening products. Even multi-national brands have introduced whitening products to increase their profits.

Many people have asked us where colorism comes from. Our conclusion is that it has its roots in several cultural streams. One major stream, colonialism, has played a major role in propagating this bias. In the colonial world, the *Sahib* (lord or landowner) was always white. White skin became synonymous with affluence, power, and position. In addition, slavery, apartheid, and other repressive institutions contributed to the devaluation of people based on their skin color.

India is believed to be comprised primarily from two races, the Aryan and the Dravidian. People of Aryan origin are generally light skinned. Those of the Dravidian decent are usually dark. To make matters worse, we have the caste system endorsed by the *Manusmriti*, an ancient Hindu legal document on social behavior possibly coined by a high-caste Brahmin. Unfortunately, the *Manusmriti* was one of the first Sanskrit texts translated during the British rule of India, by Sir William Jones in 1794.

The *Manusmriti* was used by the British colonial government to formulate the Hindu law and codes of conduct for the country, thus endorsing discriminatory practices of all kinds. For example, some Aryan mantras give them the right to discriminate against the *Shudras* (literally *slave* in Hindi), Hinduism's lowest caste, who are generally believed to be dark-skinned.

It is shocking to see how different cultures endorse and practice colorism, from the Philippines to Tanzania. A recent documentary on the issue shared the heartrending story of Filipina businesswoman Elvie Pineda, whose suffering because of her skin color included rape and abuse—which led her to launch her own skin-whitening company! Then there is the story of people who hunt albino Africans for their body parts to perform a ritual that is believed will enable a person to be prosperous.

TAKING ON THE ELEPHANT: DARK IS BEAUTIFUL

AS WE BECAME MORE and more aware of the devastation wreaked by colorism, we realized no one was addressing this issue, or even remotely acknowledging it as a social evil. So we decided to say NO to skin-color bias in a land that defines beauty in fair shades of skin tone.

In 2009, WOW launched *Dark Is Beautiful* (DISB)–an awareness campaign designed to draw attention to the unjust effects of colorism as well as to celebrate the beauty and diversity of all skin tones. DISB equips people to understand what colorism is, how it affects them, and what they can do to fight against its crippling effects.

As it is possible this is your first exposure to the issue of skin-color bias, allow me to share DISB's purpose, goals, and values:

Purpose

Dark Is Beautiful aims to instigate and inspire change in traditional attitudes, perceptions, and definitions of beauty, while bringing to the forefront the issue of skin-color bias across various cultures. In keeping with WOW's core beliefs, the primary mission behind the campaign is to help people celebrate *Beauty Beyond Color* and to live up to their full potential as they recognize their innate value, worth, and significance.

Goals

The *Dark Is Beautiful* campaign works towards putting an end to skin-color bias. We demand a world where all skin shades are valued and respected. We prevent skin-color discrimination by:

- Challenging traditional perceptions of beauty
- Stimulating responsible advertising & media endorsements
- Challenging discriminatory practices based on skin color
- Helping people to overcome the effects of skin-color bias through counselling and training
- Lobbying for legislative changes to protect the dignity of, and respect for, people of all skin shades

Values

- We value all people based on their innate worth. Skin color, physical features, caste, social standing, or ethnic origins do not determine a person's worth.
- We do not endorse cultural or traditional practices that strip people of their freedom and dignity based on their skin color.
- We believe in showing our discontent with or disapproval of skin-color bias in a respectful and peaceful way.

- We do not believe in or approve of violence, vulgarity, or unethical practices to achieve the campaign's goals.

- We do not believe in judging people for existing attitudes towards skin color, but seek to promote change of attitude through discussion, dialogue, petitions, and partnerships.

- We believe that change is possible. Those who have overlooked or endorsed the issue of skin color bias can still turn around and lead the change.

- We seek to build bridges rather than to burn them. We are always open to connecting, networking, and partnering with individuals and organizations who seek to lead the change.

- We believe that media is a powerful tool which, if used rightly, can bring positive change to our societies.

- We are not against the advertising industry, but stand up for change towards responsible advertising.

- We believe in building unity in diversity, and endorse the celebration of all skin tones–from white and wheatish to dark and dusky.

LAUNCHING THE CAMPAIGN

"WELL, WE HAVE STARTED DISB. Now what do we do?"

We were brainstorming how to get people on board with our cause. In doing so, we had to face some hard facts: People were not inclined to openly face the issue of skin-color bias. In a complex society like ours, colorism can be considered superficial in comparison to other problems. Plus, since it has to do with one's appearance, it is a very personal issue.

Many people were against the idea of the campaign. They saw it as a waste of time in light of the graver issues that surrounded us. But to me, colorism *had* to be addressed. The fact that no one was standing up to it revealed its actual power in our culture. So despite the negative feedback, we decided to take the bull by the horns.

The next challenge was to find a way for people to express their thoughts on the issue. We are a culture that loves the arts. So our team decided that allowing people to use the arts as their means of expression would be a better way to introduce the campaign, rather than being preachy about it.

The result was *Beauty Beyond Color*, designed as a creative arts contest. Through a very small classified ad, we solicited contributions in different artistic categories, including photography, painting, poetry, and short story. We asked for entries that would illustrate and describe the beauty of color in all its various shades. Winners in each category would receive awards and their work would be displayed in an exhibit arranged with the British Consulate in Chennai, which sponsors many public artistic exhibitions.

We placed the ad, hoped for a few entries in each category, and presumed no one would even notice the ad. Imagine our shock when we returned to find ourselves wading through hundreds of entries! The response was incredible. In a span of just two weeks, we received at least 300 entries for each category.

Public interest swelled when the *Beauty Beyond Color* exhibit opened at the British Consulate. The media gave extensive coverage to our awards ceremony and to the exhibit itself. The next thing we knew, DISB was being featured on television, radio, and newspapers. Then the Internet took over–and DISB went viral.

TAKING ON THE
COSMETICS INDUSTRY—AND BOLLYWOOD

SINCE THE INITIAL *Beauty Beyond Color* campaign, DISB has worked proactively to not only increase awareness of skin-color bias, but to tackle propagators of colorism head on.

In 2013, we launched a petition against Emami, a leading Indian cosmetics company. Their fairness product *Fair and Handsome* featured as its endorser one of India's favorite Bollywood actors, Shah Rukh Khan. In the advertisement, Khan throws a tube of the skin-whitening product to a young boy in the fan gallery, suggesting to him he will get more out of life if he is fair (white).

DISB collected over 27,000 signatures protesting the advertisement's message, which we then sent to the Emami, its advertising agency, and Shah Rukh Khan himself. We asked them to take down the ad and, rather than promote skin-color bias, help us lead the change towards the celebration of all skin tones. We also scheduled a march upon Emami's headquarters in Mumbai to bring public attention to our petition.

At Emami headquarters, they worried that our demonstration might turn violent. Even though we made it clear that our protest would be peaceful, they sent riot police to surround us wherever we went. When we handed our petitions in to Emami company executives, they invited me to travel to Kolkata the following week to meet with the General Manager of the company. A one-hour meeting with him yielded no results. "The whole world is after fairness," he told me. "Why should I take the ad down?" "In that case," I replied, "we will continue our campaigning."

We continued our campaign, and public support began to grow. Finally, in 2014, the Advertising Standards Council of India—for the first time ever—introduced a set of *Advertising Guidelines for Fairness Products*:

■ Advertising should not communicate any discrimination as a result of skin colour. These ads should not reinforce negative social stereotyping on the basis of skin colour. Specifically, advertising should not directly or implicitly show people with darker skin, in a way which is widely seen as unattractive, unhappy, depressed or concerned. These ads should not portray people with darker skin, in a way which is widely seen as, at a disadvantage of any kind, or inferior, or unsuccessful in any aspect of life particularly in relation to being attractive to the opposite sex, matrimony, job placement, promotions and other prospects.

- In the pre-usage depiction of product, special care should be taken to ensure that the expression of the model/s in the real and graphical representation should not be negative in a way which is widely seen as unattractive, unhappy, depressed or concerned.

- Advertising should not associate darker or lighter colour skin with any particular socio- economic strata, caste, community, religion, profession or ethnicity.

- Advertising should not perpetuate gender based discrimination because of skin colour.

While the guidelines have not had a major impact on the tone of the ads, we are hoping that, in time, the ASCI will also ban celebrities from endorsing these products. Such a ban would have major impact in a celebrity-worshiping country like India.

Our work continues and grows. DISB is now recognized as a global movement against colorism. In 2013 alone, DISB was referred to and spoken about in over 18 countries, including the USA, UK, Canada, France, Germany, Malaysia, Indonesia, Bangladesh, Pakistan and Sri Lanka.

Since the launch of DISB, colorism has been written about, researched, and spoken of in leading universities like Harvard, Cambridge, and Yale. Leading Bollywood actors Nandita Das, Gul Panag, and Shekhar Kapoor have spoken out on behalf of DISB. Advertising gurus across India have started to follow and even support us.

Nandita Das has been one of our most effective spokespersons. In 2013, she gave a blistering take on color bias in media and entertainment: "I am shocked to see the rise in the number of fairness creams, dark actresses looking paler and paler with every film, and magazines, [billboards], films and advertisements showing only fair women. You could ask what is there to be shocked, as all this has always existed. But with more women in the work force, voicing their desires and concerns, more debate about gender equality and sensitivity, one would imagine that racism of this sort would be on the decline."

Gul Panag has offered her support for DISB: "Constantly having to make allowances for someone's skin colour can have a very damaging effect on one's personality, self-esteem and their confidence and it can breed a sense of terrible failure which doesn't really exist....Unless such [DISB] campaigns are in your face and remind you that such bias is unacceptable is when we will stop passing on the bias to the next generation."

MESSAGE TO THE CHURCH: STAND UP AND BE COUNTED

ALL OF THE PROGRESS that is being made in general society notwithstanding, what is most painful to me is to see skin-color bias still seated comfortably within our churches. As of this writing, the Church in India has not yet fully stood up against caste or colorism. These issues are down-played or ignored while people continue to suffer and live in bondage.

The full gospel is *holistic*. It does not just address abstract faith while ignoring its practice. The gospel as *Shalom* reaches into every aspect of our lives. It gives us an understanding of the world as God intended it to be. In a holistic gospel, there is a clear sense of liberation from all that is ungodly–including discriminatory attitudes and practices.

The gospel is relevant to every culture–not just in presenting who Christ is, but in showing the world how Christians can demonstrate Christlikeness in all its fullness. When we choose to ignore how the gospel impacts the evils of our cultures, we are not sharing the whole gospel.

In our churches, there can be a lot of emphasis on church attendance, Bible reading, and baptism. But seldom are we taught to rightly divide God's Word so that it impacts the way we live. This is one reason why legalism is so rampant in the Church in India today.

What will make the Christian faith truly attractive to the world is when people see how, as a community, we believers reflect God's heart. When others see the transforming power of the Cross seep into every aspect of our lives–including our cultural sins–they will be able to see the truth of Romans 12:2 made a reality:

Do not conform to the pattern of this world, but be transformed by the renewing of your mind. Then you will be able to test and approve what God's will is–his good, pleasing, and perfect will.

I am deeply grateful for the many church leaders who have supported and continue to support the DISB campaign.

Thank you. My prayer is that your support will spread like wildfire throughout the greater Church, breaking down every barrier–gender, skin color, and even caste.

Do not stay silent. Join us in our efforts to tell the world that in Christ there is neither male nor female, high caste or low caste, fair or dark–we are all one in Christ!

Every skin color is beautiful. We are all made to reflect the glory of the One who made us–in his Image!

Links to more information

Dark Is Beautiful Facebook page **bit.ly/DarkIsBeautifulFacebook**

Women of Worth Facebook page **bit.ly/womenofworthfb**

The Hindu article on the new advertising guidelines **bit.ly/newskinadrules**

The Georgia Strait article on the documentary *Hue: A Matter of Color* **bit.ly/huemoviestraight**

Business Today article on the fairness products industry **bit.ly/fairskinproducts**

Wikipedia entry for the Manu Smriti **bit.ly/manusmritiwiki**

The Advertising Standards Council of India **www.asconline.org**

Gul Panag on the *Dark Is Beautiful* Campaign (not accessible in all countries) **youtu.be/M5a57yBGqSE**

Breaking Through The Barriers

The Powerhouse Journey

JEYAKARAN EMMANUEL

If you were from Chennai and walked into one of our Powerhouse churches, you might be in for a surprise.

The worship music and style, on the one hand, could be familiar–lively, up-tempo worship songs, led by a band. But who is that woman up there, *leading* the worship? Women leading...that doesn't happen very often.

And look at some of the couples in the congregation. You know enough about the caste system, and who belongs to what caste, to recognize that some of these couples look to be from different castes. Families, linked across caste lines?

And now the worship leader is delivering a greeting. She shares how Jesus loves and regards everyone equally, no matter what gender, caste, or–*color*? You know good and well that skin-color bias is a social reality here. But look again at some of the couples and families. You see people of lighter and darker shades, together. Amazing!

So how did the Powerhouse churches come into being? It has been a journey.

DEEP ROOTS, DEEP PROBLEMS

CHENNAI IS IN South India—one of the birthplaces for the early church. It is believed that in New Testament times, St. Thomas came, ministered, was martyred, and is buried here. The Christian community here can trace its roots back two thousand years.

With roots come traditions. South India is one of the most conservative areas in our country, and perhaps the world. This runs true for both the Christian church and the society at large. India's cultures are thousands of years old, so our cultural traditions run deep. Among the many positive aspects of our cultures—love of family, valuing personal relationships, a commitment to community over the individual—run some darker strains:

The caste system. People are segregated by caste and sub-caste. The principle is that all people are created *un*equally. In India, we have people above us and people below us. And cultural practice dictates that people from different castes remain separate, especially when people from upper castes engage people from lower castes. Socializing, dining, and most especially, marrying across caste lines are taboo. For example, there are still instances of *honor killings* that can take place when a couple wishes to marry across caste lines. Members of one family, to save the "honor" of their family, will kill the prospective bride or groom from the other family. Sometimes, both the bride and groom will be killed—a family will even kill their own son or daughter.

Honor killings are not an occasional outrage or a practice confined to rural villages. They are a nationwide scourge. Chennai is a megacity located in the southern state of Tamil Nadu. We are home to multi-national corporations and an exploding IT sector. We consider ourselves to be modern, progressive, and sophisticated. "Honor killings are something one hears about only in the rural North," we say. Yet just a few weeks before this writing, two such honor killings took place in Tamil Nadu–one horrifically captured on video and made viral on the Internet. The lethal consequences of the caste system are very much alive and with us today.

Oppression of women. India is a male-dominated society. Women are seen as lower status from the moment they are conceived in the womb. This discriminatory view has deep impact on women in our culture–from before birth all the way through childhood, education, employment, marriage, and beyond.

Two of the ghastliest consequences of the low view of women in India are the practices of *female feticide* and *female infanticide*.

Go to any community in India–from megacities to small villages–and you will find ultrasound clinics. In those clinics, you will see signs that say: *Determination of Sex of Foetus by Ultra Scan or any other Diagnostic Procedure is a punishable offence as per PCPNDT Act 1994 and it is not practiced here.*

Why those signs? Because some prospective parents want to get an ultrasound not to check on the health of the fetus, but to determine the gender of the baby. If they discover the fetus is a girl, they will have it aborted. And even though this practice is illegal, this testing is still clandestinely done.

It gets worse. Some families, when a girl baby is born, will kill the baby and cast it into the trash. A North Indian friend of mine recalls walking to school as a child. He was a Delhi slum kid; his path to school ran alongside the drainage canal. "There were many mornings that, as I walked, I would see the body of a baby girl," he told me. "It had been thrown into the canal or along the shoreline, left to rot or as food for the stray dogs."

Color bias. Skin color has great importance here. Fair skin is valued, while darker skin is shunned. While this applies to both genders, this is especially true for women.

Go into any large store in a city like Chennai and, in the cosmetics section, you will find dozens of skin-whitening products. It is a multi-billion-dollar industry.

GROWING UP IN TRADITION

I AM CHENNAI born and raised. While I grew up in an Anglican church background, my faith came alive when I accepted Christ at 16 years old. As a young Christian, I began my spiritual journey in churches that reflected the surrounding culture—legalistic and steeped in tradition. And I quickly realized that the Church in India practiced the same caste, gender, and color discrimination as the general society.

An example is my family and community. Though we are Christian, we are also part of a caste–the Nadars. Nadars pride ourselves on our caste pedigree. We would normally choose our husband or wife only from among fellow Nadar families.

I vividly remember a couple I knew when I was a teenager. They were both Christians, from Christian families. They were also both leaders in the local youth ministry, which is where they met. They fell in love and wished to marry.

One would think this would be an ideal match for their Christian parents. Not only were the boy and girl both following Christ, they were in ministry together. But the boy's family was Nadar–the girl's family was not. Despite their shared faith in Christ, shared commitment to ministry, and shared dreams for a life together, the boy's family crushed any possibility of a marriage. The love shared by the heartbroken couple was no match for the power of caste bias.

CHOKING ON TRADITION

FOR SOME REASON, even though I had been raised in such a culture, my faith caused me to question what I saw. How could the Church engage in perspectives and practices that seemed antithetical to the Scriptures? Why did God's people mirror the same cultural biases that surrounded them? Where was the transformational power of the gospel?

While I was not a theologian then (nor am I one now), the core values of Scripture seemed plain enough. Does not creation itself begin with the affirmation that all people are made in God's image–equally sharing the precious identity given them by God, without any regard for caste, gender, or other distinctions?

> *So God created mankind in his own image,*
> *in the image of God he created them;*
> *male and female he created them.*
>
> Genesis 1:27

And does not Paul, in his letter to the Galatians, make it clear that in Christ, all humanity are not just equally valued, but actually related–literally one another's siblings through faith in Jesus?

> *So in Christ Jesus you are all children of God through faith, for all*
> *of you who were baptized into Christ have clothed yourselves with*
> *Christ. There is neither Jew nor Gentile, neither slave nor free,*
> *nor is there male and female, for you are all one in Christ Jesus.*
>
> Galatians 3:26-28

I began to have a holy disgust for the bias and discrimination I saw all around me. And even as a teenager, I made a vow to myself: when the time came, I would marry outside of my caste.

A NEW COMMUNITY, A TIME OF TRANSFORMATION

AFTER MY UNIVERSITY studies in engineering, I moved to Mumbai to take a job. There I connected with a church that transformed my faith.

Bombay Baptist Church (now known as Gateway Ministries International) was a large, well-known congregation. I had heard many good things about Stanley Mehta, their senior pastor. My first Sunday in Mumbai, I made my way to services at BBC. Little did I know what I was in for.

Some years before, BBC had experienced a charismatic renewal. This renewal, along with the leadership of Pastor Stanley, created a commitment to empower all believers to find and function in the giftings God had given them.

While this might sound innocuous today, this was radical in India 20 years ago. The leadership tradition I was familiar with from South India was *the pastor as guru*. He had all power, ran everything in the church, and expected the congregation to attend, listen, and give. Ministry was to be left to the ordained professionals.

So imagine my shock when I arrived at BBC and tried to get acquainted. "What are the titles of your staff?" I asked. "We don't have titles here." "But how am I supposed to know who the ministers are?" I replied. "Every person here is a minister," I was told. "Some minister as church staff, but God has everyone in ministry, somewhere."

My shock increased when I met Pastor Stanley for the first time. I hadn't quite completed my greeting of "Hello,

Pastor, my name is–," when he stopped me. "Don't call me Pastor. Call me Stan." I couldn't believe it.

Then there was the service. Where I was used to seeing the senior pastor leading every aspect of the service, leadership of the worship, prayers, announcements, Scripture reading, and more were shared by many different people, most of them laypersons. And as people began to share praises and prayer needs, I heard about men and women involved in all sorts of ministries. Serving the poor, reaching out to university students, caring for the elderly, sharing the gospel with friends in the business world... people at BBC did not just warm pews. They were making a difference for Christ in the real world.

PRACTICING WHAT THEY PREACHED—IN MARRIAGE

THE NEXT THING I noticed was that there were inter-caste couples in the congregation. There was a spirit of Christian community that transcended traditional caste barriers. This was a church that not only preached the unity of the body of Christ, but practiced it where the rubber meets the road in India–in marriage.

Pastor Stanley had a phrase he used often: *"Casteism is an insult to the blood of Jesus."* It was transformational to be part of a church that did not just say these words, but lived them out.

Coming from a legalistic church background, for the very first time I experienced church as a grace-filled community of unconditional love and acceptance. These glimpses of

God's amazing grace at BBC began my lifelong journey from legalism and empty religious tradition to freedom in Christ.

The two years I spent in this church revolutionized my own vision for what church could be. When I had the opportunity to take a new job back in my home area, I returned with the intent to form a community of young people who would model the values I had absorbed from Bombay Baptist Church. I journeyed back to Chennai with the vision to begin the community that would eventually become Powerhouse.

A NEW WRINKLE—MY SPOUSE

AT THIS TIME, God added a new element into my journey. Kavitha was a beautiful, intelligent, dynamic, godly woman. She was also from another caste.

Normally, a caste-conscious Nadar would not stoop to marry someone from any other caste. But my attraction to Kavitha coincided with my vow to marry outside of my caste. I was excited to see how God had directed my path to such a fantastic young woman.

What I had not anticipated was Kavitha's perspective on the full equality of believers, including women. She was committed to the priesthood of *all* believers. Her understanding of the gospel meant women as well as men were equally valued by God and equally gifted in all areas of service, not just roles traditionally ascribed to women. Her prayer was for a husband who would fully support her in her calling to empower and release women into their full potential and destiny.

While I considered myself to be quite progressive, I didn't realize my understanding of the role of women was limited. The traditional image of a husband in my context led me to think a wife is someone whom God brings into a man's life to support his vision.

To my embarrassment, I became aware of this dynamic on our very first date. For some reason, I thought in this first encounter I should spell out all of my vision and dreams for the future (without any regard for what might be on her mind and heart). When I'd finished, I concluded, "What I need to know is, will you submit to and support my vision that God has given me?" This was on the first date!

Kavitha was taken aback, but quickly recovered. She began to share passionately about the vision God had given her. With equal passion, she shared her vision of a husband and wife who supported each other's visions. Needless to say, it was a lively first date!

But from this first awkward encounter, we began to explore our perspectives and values as we got to know one another better. I began to realize why the equality of both men and women was crucial if the priesthood of all believers was to become real in the Church. And Kavitha's awareness of the issues of color, and their devastating impact on women, opened my eyes to this area as well. Together, our vision for Powerhouse began to expand as we gradually learned how to support each other's visions while we also pursued our own.

POWERHOUSE TODAY:
CASTE, GENDER, AND COLOR BLIND

TODAY, POWERHOUSE IS a network of five churches in the Chennai area. In many ways, our look, approach, and style are not unlike many progressive churches seeking to reach younger, educated members of a large urban community. But in three key areas, Powerhouse seeks to make the transformational power of the gospel real to members and seekers alike:

Inter-caste marriage. Powerhouse supports marriages between believers regardless of their caste backgrounds. We have many such inter-caste marriages in our congregations.

Maintaining this position has subjected us to criticism and pressure. I have had many encounters with Christian families irate over the prospect of their son or daughter marrying outside of their caste. Faith notwithstanding, marriage still comprises the acid test of one's views on caste in our society.

At this point, I need to explain another toxic aspect of our marriage system—the system of *dowry*. In our society, a bride is seen as a financial burden. When she marries, she becomes not just the property of the husband's family, but their responsibility. She is another mouth to feed, clothe, and house. (It is the reality of a female child being a financial burden to their family that fuels the practices of female feticide and female infanticide.)

Dowry is the means by which the bride's family pays tribute to the groom's family to compensate them for the financial burden they are taking on. In addition to bearing all of the expenses for the wedding, the bride's family is expected to make a substantial "gift" to the groom's family. These "gifts" can be valuables such as cash, gold, and jewelry, assets such as animals and property, or a combination of gifts.

The pressure of dowry can continue after marriage. Grooms' families unhappy with the amount of dowry will badger the brides' families for even more tribute. More horrifically, a young wife will die in a "kitchen accident" or be found dead from suicide. The groom's family then begin the search for another bride and more dowry.

Tragically, dowry is also practiced in the church. But at Powerhouse, we have stood against this practice. We marry couples only when their families have promised that no dowry is involved with the match.

This commitment to open, dowry-free marriage has not been easy to maintain. But we have stood the course, believing this is the path God has put us on for the sake of the gospel. And he has honored our commitment.

The priesthood of all believers. In Powerhouse, women serve in all positions of leadership. Women lead worship, preach from the pulpit, serve communion, and administer baptism. In fact, almost half of our teaching team are women.

Our commitment to release women to function in any role God has called them to comes out of our conviction that leadership is determined by gifting and calling, not gender. While we are well aware of the theological tensions that divide the body of Christ over the issue of women in leadership, we choose to take this path with the simple assurance from the Scriptures such as the passages we referred to earlier (Genesis 1:27, Galatians 3:26-28).

Again, I am no theologian. But I believe the whole of Scripture speaks of a God who loves all of his creation equally and calls for his people not to seek power or titles, but to love, serve, and support one another. Paul captures this beautifully in his letter to the Philippians:

Therefore if you have any encouragement from being united with Christ, if any comfort from his love, if any common sharing in the Spirit, if any tenderness and compassion, then make my joy complete by being like-minded, having the same love, being one in spirit and of one mind. Do nothing out of selfish ambition or vain conceit. Rather, in humility value others above yourselves, not looking to your own interests but each of you to the interests of the others.

In your relationships with one another, have the same mindset as Christ Jesus: Who, being in very nature God, did not consider equality with God something to be used to his own advantage;

rather, he made himself nothing
by taking the very nature of a servant,
being made in human likeness.
And being found in appearance as a man,
he humbled himself
by becoming obedient to death–
even death on a cross!

Philippians 2:1-8

Early on, we decided that, rather than put our energies into explaining or advocating our position on the full participation of women, we would just practice it. That has been our approach since the beginning. God has empowered all believers; our members, men and women alike, live out their giftings as they have been given by God.

From message to movement. Kavitha has taken this practice and expanded it into an effective movement. Women of Worth (WOW) is dedicated to empowering women to be the best they can be. First started as a women's fellowship in the church, WOW has expanded to become an international NGO–advocating the value and worth of women to a global constituency.

WOW has since birthed a groundbreaking movement to tackle the scourge of skin-color bias. Dark Is Beautiful (DISB) helps women (and more recently, men) understand their full value as human beings regardless of the color of their skin. DISB has gone viral, with hundreds of thousands of people connecting with DISB through social media and spreading the message of *beauty beyond color*. [Read about WOW, DISB, and Kavitha's journey in pursuing the call God gave her in "Dark Is Beautiful," p. 177.–Ed.]

A REFORMATION IN INDIA—AND THE WORLD

AS I INTERACT and work with pastors and churches across India, I am convinced that one of the greatest barriers to the church's ability to impact our society is the condition of the church itself. As the Father of our nation, Mahatma Gandhi, put it candidly, "I like your Christ, I do not like your Christians. Your Christians are so unlike your Christ."

Gandhi's words ring painfully true. But there is hope. I believe God is inspiring a radical reformation for the Church in India–a reformation that will eliminate all oppressive and discriminatory practices from our midst. The Church in India will become a place of love and acceptance of all people, just as God created them.

Like India, the global church faces the same challenges. We all are susceptible to incorporating the oppressive and discriminatory practices found in our respective societies into our church cultures. When we do this, we cripple our Christian witness. "What difference does Jesus make?" people will ask. "You live just like us." And they will be right.

My prayer is that we will allow the power of the gospel to transform us where it counts–in the dark crevasses of bias, prejudice, injustice, and oppression. Then, *truly*, we can fulfill the call Jesus gave to us in his famous Sermon on the Mount:

"You are the light of the world. A town built on a hill cannot be hidden. Neither do people light a lamp and put it under a bowl. Instead they put it on its stand, and it gives light to everyone in the house. In the same way, let your light shine before others, that they may see your good deeds and glorify your Father in heaven."

Matthew 5:14-16

The Strangers In Our Midst

Migrant Worker Church

"BARTHOLOMEW" AND "TITUS"

Editor's note: Because these leaders live and minister in a country where repression and persecution of Christians is an issue, we have disguised their identities and locations.

Sunday morning. It is time for church. Our congregation gathers at our place of worship. Hundreds of people are converging from the surrounding neighborhoods. This same thing is happening in congregations all over the city.

But these congregations are different. Our meeting places are on the outskirts of the city, tucked away in crowded slums. Some of our meeting places are at or near the municipal dumps. And technically, our members do not even exist. They are migrant workers, immigrants from the countryside. They are poor, they are struggling, and they are illegal. And they are our mission field.

THE GREAT MIGRATION

THE STORY OF OUR country has been turbulent. For decades, our government severely restricted the movement of people within the country.

In the 1980s, this began to change. A concerted campaign to improve the economic condition of the people meant that labor was needed in our major cities. The government began to open up the paths to internal migration.

People from the impoverished countryside began to flood into our major cities, looking to fill this need for labor. They sought to escape economically hopeless environments in their home villages, seeking a better life in the city for themselves and their families.

This migration increased in the subsequent decades. More and more people poured into the cities; by the turn of the century, we had experienced a major urbanization of our country's population.

Migrants from the country took on the dirty jobs no one else wanted. They served as day laborers, taking the odd jobs that were available. They peddled fruits, meats, and vegetables. And they worked as scavengers, digging through the municipal dumps for recyclable materials to sell.

These migrants helped to fill the need for laborers, but they also generated tensions between themselves and the urban residents. Huge cultural, ethnic, and economic gaps divided these populations. City dwellers resented this tidal wave of what they saw as uneducated, uncouth, and unruly laborers.

PRESENT DAY: SATURATION AND STRUGGLE

TODAY, OUR CITIES ARE saturated with economic migrants. They are largely uneducated and poor. And their lives are fraught with struggle.

Workers struggle just to survive in an environment where they can be easily exploited by unscrupulous employers. Parents struggle with how to best care for their children. Many leave their children behind with grandparents in the countryside, breaking up their families. Other parents bring their children with them to the city. But in the city, there are no schools available for their children. So these children end up working alongside their parents or wandering loose, thus continuing the cycle of lack of education and accompanying poverty.

Worst of all, due to our country's laws, migrant workers hold no legal status in the cities where they live and work–even if they have lived there for decades. Due to their lack of legal status, they do not qualify for any of the benefits available to city residents, such as access to health care or to schools for their children.

So migrant workers and their families have created a hybrid, third culture in our country. They do not belong to the city, nor do they belong to their home villages. Migrant workers are essentially stateless. This hybrid status has created a sense of identity confusion and alienation among migrant workers. They are distanced from their resentful urban neighbors, distanced from their friends and relatives in their home villages, and ultimately distanced from their own sense of self.

THE SURPRISE: MIGRANT WORKERS' SPIRITUAL STATUS

A SURPRISING ASPECT of the migrant worker culture is their spiritual status. Many of these workers come to the cities as Christians, having been raised in Christian families or having converted to Christ in their home villages. And the turmoil involved in migrating to and living in the city has created an openness to the gospel among many migrant workers. For all of its difficulties, the migrant worker communities are a fruitful mission field for Christian workers who are willing to engage these communities.

PREPARATION FOR OUR CALL:
GROWING UP IN THE PROVINCES

WE BOTH FEEL GOD prepared us for migrant worker ministry from our births. We both grew up in countryside provinces. "Titus" came from a second-generation Christian family; "Bartholomew's" parents became Christians when he was a baby, following his mother's healing from demonic possession through the prayer of believers.

In 2001, we both happened to come to our country's capital city to study at seminary, ending up in the same class. The professor of that class was committed to the idea of Christians making a difference in their communities. He challenged the students to get out from the four walls of the seminary and minister to the surrounding community.

God used that professor's challenge to spark the beginning of a call in us both. We began to explore possible ways that we could serve in our local community. We tried various ministries (for example, reaching out to university students), but nothing seemed to fit. Then we made two discoveries. First, we were made aware of a migrant worker community located very near to our professor's office. Second, a friend who was running a school for the children of migrant workers offered to connect us to this community.

FEELING OUR WAY TO A CALLING

OUR JOURNEY INTO migrant worker ministry was, for us, almost like "feeling" our way to a calling. There were three reasons for this.

First, we were exploring without a sense of direction. The educational system in our country emphasizes conformity, rote learning, and achieving high test scores. It does not encourage students to develop their own sense of direction. So for us, the act of exploration was a step into unknown territory. We knew we wanted to find where God wanted us to serve, but we did not know how to do so. Our exploration had a sense of aimlessness. It was as we became aware of the migrant worker community, their needs, and how they might be reached that we became aware of a sense of call.

The second reason was more an affirmation of how God had uniquely equipped us for migrant worker ministry. Because we were both from the provinces, we already had language and cultural connections with the incoming migrant workers. God had given us natural ways to connect and build relationships with them that urban residents did not have.

Third, God led us into migrant worker ministry at a key historical time for our country. We began to reach out to migrant workers as they were swarming into the capitol city, creating turmoil and tensions for migrant workers and urban residents alike. We could sense God had prepared us for such a time as this.

SCRIPTURE AND THE STRANGER

AS WE GREW INTO our sense of calling, we began to see how the Bible speaks to the concept of reaching people like our migrant workers: poor, displaced, strangers in their own land, consigned to the "dirty work" of society and then despised for it.

From the original books of Moses, God gives us direct commands as to how we are to treat those we consider strangers and foreigners:

And you are to love those who are foreigners, for you yourselves were foreigners in Egypt.

Deuteronomy 10:19

When you reap the harvest of your land, do not reap to the very edges of your field or gather the gleanings of your harvest. Leave them for the poor and for the foreigner residing among you.

Leviticus 23:22

In Isaiah, chapter 58:6-7, we are given a mandate as to the "fasting" that God is looking for from his people:

Is not this the kind of fasting I have chosen:
to loose the chains of injustice
and untie the cords of the yoke,
to set the oppressed free
and break every yoke?
Is it not to share your food with the hungry
and to provide the poor wanderer with shelter–
when you see the naked, to clothe them,
and not to turn away from your own flesh and blood?

Jesus' life and work was a living demonstration of reaching out to the downtrodden and unloved–his fellowship with tax collectors, his willingness to engage the Samaritan woman, his calling of the unruly group of fishermen who became his disciples. Our Lord summed up his call to serve the poor and struggling in this passage from Matthew:

"When the Son of Man comes in his glory, and all the angels with him, he will sit on his glorious throne. All the nations will be gathered before him, and he will separate the people one

from another as a shepherd separates the sheep from the goats.
He will put the sheep on his right and the goats on his left.

"Then the King will say to those on his right, 'Come, you who
are blessed by my Father; take your inheritance, the kingdom
prepared for you since the creation of the world. For I was
hungry and you gave me something to eat, I was thirsty and you
gave me something to drink, I was a stranger and you invited
me in, I needed clothes and you clothed me, I was sick and you
looked after me, I was in prison and you came to visit me.'

"Then the righteous will answer him, 'Lord, when did
we see you hungry and feed you, or thirsty and give you
something to drink? When did we see you a stranger and
invite you in, or needing clothes and clothe you? When
did we see you sick or in prison and go to visit you?'

"The King will reply, 'Truly I tell you, whatever you did for one of
the least of these brothers and sisters of mine, you did for me.'"

Matthew 25:31-40

MIGRANT WORKER CHURCH:
BIRTH, GROWTH, DEVELOPMENT

BEGINNING IN 2001, we embarked on a path of experimenting and learning. We began by planting four churches in migrant worker neighborhoods. Each church was planted and developed through a four-step process:

- Planting the church
- Teaching our new congregants

- Pastoring and shepherding our congregants

- Investing in holistic ministry–caring for our congregants' physical, emotional, and other needs in addition to their spiritual needs

These churches developed and grew much faster than we anticipated. After a whirlwind first three years, we began to solidify the work. As we continued to minister and lead the churches over the next few years, we also:

- Moved into the migrant worker neighborhoods so we could live close to the churches that had been planted

- Recruited and trained students from the seminary to serve as interns, providing us with much-needed help

- Became more involved in our congregants' personal lives–attending graduations, officiating marriages, and celebrating with new parents as they began their families

GETTING INVOLVED IN THE DIFFICULT ISSUES OF LIFE

AS WE GOT MORE involved in the lives of our members, we began to face difficult issues. We had to learn to come alongside our brothers and sisters as they faced heart-rending decisions in their lives.

Some years ago, a worker arrived in our city with his son, daughter-in-law, and their child, all followers of Christ. Until recently, our country has had a one-child policy. But this couple became pregnant with their second child. And they soon learned this child, a girl, had Down Syndrome, which would result in severe repercussions for a poor family such as theirs. Many of their relatives counseled that the couple get an abortion. But the worker, the girl's grandfather, believed that she was a gift from God and should be allowed to live.

The girl was born. Since her birth, she has suffered from many health problems, resulting in frequent visits to the hospital. This has resulted in a major financial burden on the family. The family has had to struggle with the tensions and pressures created by the situation in which they find themselves.

Recently, this family has relocated to another city. Pastor "Titus" (their minister when they were in the capitol city) visits the family at least once a year to minister to them in their difficult journey.

In the countryside, people are involved in one another's lives. But in the urban culture of our country, one would not get involved in the personal issues of a family, even in the context of a church. This would be considered the family's private business–even the decision whether or not to abort a pregnancy.

The urban dynamic of isolation and privacy has permeated into the migrant worker communities. But in the migrant worker church, we are trying to re-establish this kind of involvement in one another's lives. We are working to rebuild the practice of caring for one another, especially in tough times, back into the life of our congregations.

STRONG GROWTH, BIG CHALLENGES

THE NEXT TWO YEARS were a period of strong growth. Nine more churches were planted, and the number of new believers and church members swelled. But even with such dynamic growth, we had settled into comfortable routines and rituals without even realizing it.

In 2007, we were shaken out of our rut by our former seminary professor. He cared deeply about the migrant workers in his area and decided to become involved in the ministry. He quickly saw the rut within which we had settled; just as quickly, he challenged us to get out of our comfort zones. He had ideas for how we could expand the reach and effectiveness of the migrant worker ministry:

- First, go to the migrant workers' home villages in the countryside several times each year.

- Second, train local workers in those villages to lead their countryside churches.

- Third, provide assistance to these workers and the countryside churches as they struggle to maintain life and vitality in the midst of their young people leaving their villages for the lure of the cities.

This professor also had a bold new vision–for migrant worker pastors like us to reach out and connect with urban pastors in our city. This was a real stretch out of our comfort zones. As migrant worker pastors, and migrants ourselves from the countryside, we felt insecure about reaching out to big-city pastors. Just as migrant workers feel rejected by urban residents, those of us in migrant worker ministry can feel rejected by the pastors of these same urban residents.

To our pleasant surprise, God honored our professor's bold vision and our tentative efforts. As we began to reach out to urban pastors, good relationships were developed. Much good healing and understanding took place between ministers who previously had no relationship.

Finally, this professor challenged us to move away from the "do it all ourselves" model of ministry and toward the development of ministry teams. He could foresee the path to burnout we were forging, and he encouraged us toward the benefits of shared leadership and ministry.

These ministry teams have produced many benefits. Among them, they have caused us to have to clarify our vision, core values, agenda, policies, and more. Our migrant worker ministry is less a work of two people and more a collective effort. That said, these ministry teams remain a work in progress.

OUTGROWING OUR OLD MODELS

AS WE MOVED forward, we began to outgrow our original models. During our original church planting efforts, three families became the core of our leadership. These families developed the ministry along certain lines, and along certain models. As the work grew and our network expanded, we realized the need to expand: both the range of models for our work, and for our work to grow beyond the control of just those three families. In our culture, navigating this kind of transition is a sensitive process.

We were also learning the limitations of trying to apply urban church models to migrant worker communities. Urban congregations are usually more educated and take an intellectual approach to the Christian life. They want more complexity and detail in their faith and practice and want more opportunities for lay people to participate in ministry.

Migrant worker congregations, on the other hand, are usually less educated and take a pragmatic approach to the Christian life. They look to God and to their leadership for simple, practical guidance with basic life issues (e.g., making a living, food, shelter, and healing from physical and spiritual illnesses). They want direct teaching from their leaders and do not see themselves as participants in ministry, at least initially.

We have also learned that pastors for migrant worker churches *must* come from the migrant worker community. Without the shared understanding of migrant worker life, culture, and language, the pastor will unable to be able to successfully connect with migrant worker congregants. At the same time, migrant worker pastors need to be connected with urban church pastors. This connection is vital for migrant worker pastors to grow and stretch in ways that help their spiritual, personal, and ministry development.

POTENTIAL BREAKTHROUGH

THE CONTINUING GROWTH of the migrant worker churches created the need for more leadership and co-workers than could be provided by just the three founding families. Also, more seminary graduates were graduating from school with a call to migrant worker and countryside church ministry. The challenge with this increasing call was that migrant worker and countryside churches are usually too poor to support a full-time pastor.

To address these issues, in 2010 God gave us a vision to create a one-year study program in the city. Each year, 10 to 12 students from the countryside who demonstrate leadership potential are invited to spend a year living, studying, and ministering in the capitol city. All costs for this program are underwritten by the urban migrant worker ministry community.

These students are taught by experienced migrant worker pastors and given the chance to develop practical skills in migrant worker ministry. At the conclusion of the year, any of these students who feel so called can stay on and continue to minister to the migrant worker community.

This program is the prime driver for our current focus: to see how we can integrate the historical ministry models of the three pioneer families with those of the study program graduates. This is the sensitive work that continues to this day.

PRESENT-DAY EMPHASES

CURRENTLY, WE ARE investing in three emphases: spreading the gospel, pastoring existing churches, and planting new churches. Within these emphases, we are:

- Training and equipping more leaders as churches expand

- Investing in Sunday school

- Trying to reach youth (primarily second-generation migrant workers): Reaching these youth is very challenging because of the family dynamics experienced by migrant worker children. Typical youth ministry models do not work with these young people.

This past year, we have begun a new stretch. We have sent two couples to another major city in our country to begin ministry and church planting in the migrant worker community in that city.

MIGRANT WORKER MINISTRY: LOOKING INTO THE FUTURE

AS WE SEEK GOD'S direction for the future of the migrant worker ministry to which he has called us, we are aware of some significant trends.

First, the wave of migration to the cities is slowing. The major cities in our country are now saturated with migrant workers. Employment opportunities for migrant workers are diminishing. And the government is working to reduce the migrant worker population and send these workers back to their home villages or to other cities.

Second, the increasing costs of urban living are making it more difficult for migrant workers to survive, even when they can find employment. Finally, our government, since the beginning of the urbanization wave, has intentionally restricted educational opportunities for migrant worker children. This lack of access to education means that a move to the city by countryside parents does not necessarily mean a better life for their children.

We are now seeing a New Migration. Workers are leaving our four major cities and relocating to second- and third-level cities where there are still economic opportunities. The urban migration continues, albeit along new geographic lines.

Those of us in migrant worker ministry are strategizing how we can follow their footsteps. Trained countryside leaders are following the migrant workers to their new locations. We are also sending pastors from our four major cities to relocate to these second- and third-level cities to plant new migrant worker churches.

We are very early in implementing these new strategies, and are already learning some early lessons. We have found that it is easier for countryside pastors to relocate to larger cities; conversely, we have learned that it is more difficult for pastors from our four major cities to relocate to the second- and third-level cities.

GENERATIONAL TRANSITIONS, NEW APPROACHES

IN ADDITION TO the geographical shifts, we are experiencing a transition to a new generation of migrant workers. The first generation of migrant workers has matured; we are now working with a second generation, comprised of both the children of the first generation of migrant workers and young people who are making their way to the cities.

The first generation of migrant workers had certain characteristics. They came to the city as adults. Their only goal was to make money. They had a simple approach to living. And they always intended to return to their home village, no matter how many years (or decades) they lived in the city.

This second generation has different characteristics. Unlike the first generation, these second-generation workers were born in the city or came to the city as young children. They identify more with their urban peers than with those from their former villages. Their inclination is to stay in the city, as they would have great difficulty in adjusting back to country life. That said, they struggle with their identities. They are city dwellers, but not accepted by the city; they are from the country, but cannot relate anymore to their village roots. Their collective cry is, "Where do I belong?"

Reaching this second generation has required us to be more creative in our approaches. This generation is more active and experience-oriented than their forbearers. To reach them, we must directly involve them in activities and experiences.

CLARIFYING OUR CALL IN THE FACE OF CHANGE

FINALLY, WE BOTH, along with others in our leadership teams, must clarify our call in the face of new choices and opportunities. Many of us are now being offered pastorates with urban churches. Accepting these calls would result in many benefits, not the least of which would be a more improved economic situation for ourselves and our families.

These opportunities are flattering and tempting. But what about our call to reach out to migrant workers? Is that still our calling? Is God moving some of us to new ministries? At this writing, many of our team leaders are struggling with such decisions.

For the two of us, we believe that God has called, and continues to call us, to follow and minister to the migrant workers. But we must be honest: obeying this call is a challenge, given the financial challenges we face as we raise growing families.

Would you pray with us and for us?

Jesus went through all the towns and villages, teaching in their synagogues, proclaiming the good news of the kingdom and healing every disease and sickness. When he saw the crowds, he had compassion on them, because they were harassed and helpless, like sheep without a shepherd. Then he said to his disciples, "The harvest is plentiful but the workers are few. Ask the Lord of the harvest, therefore, to send out workers into his harvest field."

Matthew 9:35-38

The Outreach Centre Movement

Urban Church Planting in an Age of Intolerance

DAVID DAYALAN

"Pastor, I'm sorry, but we are going to have to raise your rent."

I was sitting across from the general manager of a large building in Gurgaon, just outside of Delhi. Gurgaon Christian Fellowship (GCF), the church I pastor, had been meeting in this building for ten years. Gurgaon is a modern suburb where many of India's corporate managers and professionals live. Much of the development is recent, and the local government resists the construction of Christian churches. So GCF, like other churches in Gurgaon, rents space to use for worship, fellowship, and meetings.

Our ten years as a tenant had been smooth and peaceful. But in 2014 our country experienced a major change. After decades of dominance, the Congress party had been voted out in national elections. The Bharatiya Janata Party (BJP), preaching a hardline Hindu message sandwiched between promises to spark economic growth and clean up corruption, had won a landslide victory. BJP leaders were moving quickly to bring change–and not just political or economic change. A new wind was blowing in India.

"How much of an increase in the rent?" I asked the landlord. I was stunned when he quoted a figure that was *four times* over our current price. "I'm afraid your parking-lot privileges are no longer available," he added. And our exit time, which had been a flexible 1:00 p.m. or so? "You will need to be out of the building by 11:00 a.m. sharp," he said. Finally, he informed us, anytime we needed to use the space for a special event or midweek meeting–something that had always been included in the base rent–we would be subject to an additional charge.

DARKENING CLOUDS OVER INDIA

OVER THE PAST few years, India has entered a season of rising intolerance, not only with respect to faith and religion, but also with any views which are contrary to the hearer's own, or "offend" the hearer in any way. The most marked difference in public life is seen in the increasing rhetoric against any faiths other than the majority Hinduism.

The change in government brought in a ruling party with a clearly stated agenda of creating a *Hindu rashtra* (Hindu nation). Since then, there have been sustained attempts to restructure the government and judiciary, as well as the educational and social systems with the intent to re-Hinduize India. There has correspondingly been a rise in the oppression and outright persecution of Christians, Muslims, and others.

The sudden, negative change in GCF's relationship with our building landlord is just one example of how the drive for *Hindu rashtra* is impacting life for Christians, Muslims, and many others in my country. Here are some additional examples of the rapidly changing landscape in India:

- Businesses and corporations are now expected to provide time off for all major Hindu holidays and festivals. Yoga practice is mandatory–not just the positions and exercises as they might be practiced in the West, but also inclusion of the Hindu religious and spiritual connotations.

- At the same time, especially for government employees, Christian holidays that had been previously observed (such as Good Friday and Christmas Day) are being eliminated. In fact, Christmas Day has been renamed Good Governance Day; it is a working day for government employees.

- Christian, Muslim, and other Non-Government Organizations (NGOs), as well as Western Christian missionaries, are being placed under special scrutiny. Organizations and individuals who accept outside financial help, especially from the West, are being targeted. Organizations have been shut down; sometimes, leaders have been jailed. All the while, NGOs sponsored by Rashtriya Swayamsevak Sangh (RSS), the militant wing of the BJP party, are receiving large financial grants from the government.

- Schools have introduced three new practices for their students:

  - Practicing yoga while voicing the Hindu chant, "Oooooommmmmmmm..."

  - *Surya na maskar,* worship of the sun god. Children kneel down and prostrate themselves to this god.

  - Practice of the *gayatri* chant, a Sanskrit devotional chant from the Vedas, the Hindu religious scriptures.

Children, no matter what their faith background, are expected to participate in these exercises. In large urban schools, families who refuse to let their children do these practices can do so at the risk of their sons and daughters being taunted and ridiculed. But in village schools, children who refuse to obey can be thrown out of school altogether.

- The BJP has replaced key officials in the national school system with ideologues. They have begun rewriting the Indian curriculum–tampering with our history, falsely inserting BJP figures into our national liberation story, and infusing teaching material with a radical perspective derived from the teachings of RSS.

- At the higher-education level, the government has installed RSS operatives as "Vice Chancellors" at major universities. As they are doing in the primary and secondary systems, these ideologues are impressing their *Hindu rashtra* version of political correctness into the university environment. Administrators, professors, and students alike are all feeling the pressure.

■ Within a year of taking power, the government issued an edict that all Indians should intone a chant (*Bharat Mata Ki Jai*), which they purport to mean, "Hail Mother India." But Sikh, Muslim, and other groups pointed out that the slogan actually means, "Hail Mother Goddess." The person chanting is praising India as a deity–an amalgamation of all of the female goddesses found in Hinduism. These protests have had little avail. "If you are a patriotic Indian," the government asserts, "you will say this chant. If you do not, you are against our country."

■ This chant is just one example in a growing wave of ultra-nationalism, built around the principles of *Hindu rashtra*. Nationalism has been redefined as an unconditional embrace of the Hindu-centric perspective of the ruling party. For those who disagree, the all-encompassing accusation is anti-nationalism. Anyone who dissents from any aspect of the ultra-national wave is branded as "anti-national." No one is exempt from the pressure. Journalists, professors, and intellectuals are being swept under the rising tide of oppression.

■ In Hinduism, cows are considered sacred and are protected by law. But the veneration of cows is reaching a fevered, irrational pitch. "Cow vigilantes" are on the loose, looking for people suspected of "mistreating" cows in any way, and especially searching for those committing the ultimate sacrilege, eating beef. The "cow vigilante" mobs are growing in numbers and aggressiveness.

Physical oppression and violence are increasing. Churches have been burned, pastors and congregations harassed, "unbelievers" beaten and killed. In an incident that made global headlines, a Muslim man was lynched when BJP hardliners believed a false rumor that the man had eaten beef. While the government has distanced itself from these incidents, labeling them random acts by "fringe" elements, its tacit complicity is evident in the lack of action taken against these elements.

In this environment, traditional models of Christian faith and practice–evangelism, discipleship, worship, traditional church structure, and the like–are increasingly ineffective and irrelevant.

THE URBAN CHURCH: SPECIAL CHALLENGES

CHURCHES LOCATED IN urban, educated, upper-middle class settings must deal with additional issues. The urban centers of North India are dynamic environments that draw people from all over the country, representing many different ethnic, cultural, language, religious, and caste groups. Further, urban communities are comprised of displaced, mobile, fluid people. In such environments, the traditional church attracts *only* Christians, already looking for a church home. These churches end up catering to the needs of their members, rather than to the mission of reaching nonbelievers.

Another challenge is that in North India non-Christian populations have certain perceptions about Christians. Christians are perceived as poor and marginalized, belonging to backward (lower) castes and paid by foreigners (the West). In a society deeply entrenched in caste structure and the corresponding social implications, these perceptions–even within the church–make North Indians apprehensive about even considering Christ, if and when they are approached by Christians.

The rising popularity of humanism among the educated strata of society and its rejection of any form of religious faith poses yet another challenge to urban India. While these groups are not physically militant or oppressive, the language of intolerance is just as strong.

So for decades, we have been living in a dilemma. The institutional church in urban India has been present, visible, and active–but for the most part, among believers only. For the urban church, the problem has not been a struggle for existence. It has been a problem of *relevance*.

Ironically, the rising intolerance we see in India is a blessing in disguise for the urban church. We should have started years ago to change our approaches to outreach, discipleship, and body life. In the brave new world we now live in, we will have to change.

HOW CAN THE URBAN CHURCH REMAIN RELEVANT?

THE QUESTION FOR THE Church therefore is: *How can the urban church in North India, seeking to reach educated, upper/middle-class nonbelievers, be relevant in an environment of increasing oppression?*

The answer seems to be in changing the structure of the church that people see and experience. The change is not so much structural but *in the nature of church itself.* Rather than viewing church as an institution, we need to experience it as an organism.

This isn't new thinking. Basically, I am advocating that we bring the Church back to its roots. In the book of Acts, we are told about a growing community of new believers, learning how to live life together as Christ followers:

They devoted themselves to the apostles' teaching and to fellowship, to the breaking of bread and to prayer. Everyone was filled with awe at the many wonders and signs performed by the apostles. All the believers were together and had everything in common. They sold property and possessions to give to anyone who had need. Every day they continued to meet together in the temple courts. They broke bread in their homes and ate together with glad and sincere hearts, praising God and enjoying the favor of all the people. And the Lord added to their number daily those who were being saved.

Acts 2:42-47

All the believers were one in heart and mind. No one claimed that any of their possessions was their own, but they shared everything they had. With great power the apostles continued to testify to the resurrection of the Lord Jesus. And God's grace was so powerfully at work in them all that there were no needy persons among them. For from time to time those who owned land or houses sold them, brought the money from the sales and put it at the apostles' feet, and it was distributed to anyone who had need.

Acts 4:32-35

Now those who had been scattered by the persecution that broke out when Stephen was killed traveled as far as Phoenicia, Cyprus and Antioch, spreading the word only among Jews. Some of them, however, men from Cyprus and Cyrene, went to Antioch and began to speak to Greeks also, telling them the good news about the Lord Jesus. The Lord's hand was with them, and a great number of people believed and turned to the Lord.

Acts 11:19-21

There are of course different points of view on how the practices of the first Christians would translate into the modern world. But what is clear in the Acts narrative is that what eventually became the institutional church was first a body of people committed to one another, sharing life, worship, food, and their very possessions together, devoted to spreading the love of Christ among themselves and with others.

This turn toward "organic" Christian life and practice has already occurred in India. House church, disciple-making, and other movements are proliferating, but almost exclusively in the rural villages. In urban India, the institutional church has held sway.

So how might we translate the values of the early church into today's world–in my case, a modern, urban, dynamic environment in a nation where religious repression and persecution are on the rise?

FROM TRADITIONAL CHURCHES TO OUTREACH CENTRES

I SUGGEST WE BEGIN to move from traditional churches to Outreach Centres (OCs)–multiple numbers of smaller, highly relational communities of believers, focused on reaching non-believers. Some of the differentiators of such a church from the traditional model would be location, structure, and growth dynamics.

OCs would be location-distributed rather than location-central. Members of each OC would train together, as a community, in process-oriented interactive learning and group engagement. In the OC, the guidelines for faith and practice would be pulled from Scripture as distinct from traditions developed by the institutional church.

OCs would be organized as organic, low-structure communities rather than systematized hierarchies. In an OC, the emphasis would be on the priesthood of all believers. As the giftedness of each OC member emerges (e.g., teaching, speaking), people would be empowered in an environment where everyone is engaged in one-on-one discipleship. There would be less need for formal roles, gradually leading to a shift from paid clergy to trained lay professionals.

In this kind of a structure, church growth would be dynamic rather than systematized. The focus would be less on increasing church numbers through drives or crusades, but rather on making disciples, which by its very nature includes evangelism.

There would need to be a strong intentionality about building into one another's lives–personal, family, and workplace. Leaders in OC movements would have high trust that the Holy Spirit is in charge of a God-driven phenomenon that is beyond human, hierarchical, and structural controls.

Again, this approach simply takes us back to our roots– to the original mandate given to us by our Lord:

> *Then Jesus came to them and said, "All authority in heaven and on earth has been given to me. Therefore go and make disciples of all nations, baptizing them in the name of the Father and of the Son and of the Holy Spirit, and teaching them to obey everything I have commanded you. And surely I am with you always, to the very end of the age."*
>
> *Matthew 28:18-20*

OUTREACH CENTRES IN PROGRESS:
GURGAON CHRISTIAN FELLOWSHIP

AT GCF, THE SHIFT to Outreach Centres is already in progress. About two years ago, 15 couples were selected to become our first batch of OC group leaders. The criterion for invitation was that each person was growing in Christ, was being faithful in their current commitments, and had expressed a willingness to enter into OC training.

For twelve months, these couples gathered together for one weekend each month. Relationships were developed, giftings discovered, and plans made for the planting of future fellowships in our surrounding community. When the year was completed, these families established their respective OCs. Four teams of three couples each set up OCs in their local neighborhoods, one couple moved south to establish an OC in Bangalore, and two couples chose to remain at our main church.

Here is how it works: One midweek evening, each OC group meets together for a time of fellowship, prayer, and encouragement. They share with one another about the relationships they are nurturing with their friends, neighbors, and workplace colleagues. They plan together for the gatherings that will take place the coming Sunday.

Then, on Sundays from 9 a.m. to 11 a.m., each OC community meets together for house church–a time of worship, teaching, and prayer, led by the community itself. After that, others begin to arrive. These are the friends and neighbors the OC members have invited from their personal networks. Our OC members have sensed that these friends and neighbors could be seekers, with a potential interest in Jesus and in the Christian faith. These invited friends are there for an informal get-together–a shared meal, conversation, and the building of relationships.

The conversations are often built around topics of interest and concern to everyone–things like marriage, parenting, anger management, dealing with job stress, and so on. Within the conversational give-and-take, practical counsel from a biblical perspective can be offered, as OC members feel appropriate.

Over time, the relationships within these informal Sunday lunch groups have become quite deep, something very unusual for Indian society. OC members have found themselves providing deeper input and even counseling for their friends. They have had the chance to pray for their friends. And some of these friends are expressing interest in learning more about Jesus–many more than we have seen through the efforts of our mother church!

If and when these seekers do make a decision to become Christ followers, they will be welcomed into full participation in the OC. They will be baptized by OC leaders, join into the worship and fellowship, and continue to grow as Christ followers and full participants.

We are also working to keep our OC groups connected to the greater GCF community. Once a month, I visit with one of the OC groups on a rotating basis. It is an opportunity for me to hear firsthand about their progress and their challenges, to provide input, counsel, and additional training where appropriate, and reinforce with them that they are still connected to the greater GCF community. OC groups are of course included in all of our major GCF events. And late last fall, we had the first of what we plan to be regular gatherings, where we brought together all of our OC groups for a time of praise, prayer, encouragement, and refresher training for the ongoing ministry.

LEADER EMPOWERMENT AT A NEW LEVEL

AS THE LEAD PASTOR OF GCF, my role with our OCs is to lead successive training batches and serve as a mentor and coach to existing OCs. Over time, the OCs themselves will nurture additional mentors and coaches. Eventually, these OC-nurtured mentors and coaches will serve as the primary leaders and encouragers for the movement.

The growth of our OC leaders has been nothing short of phenomenal. These men and women are maturing into effective leaders at a much faster rate than anyone had anticipated. For me, the best part of the OC movement has been to see how quickly our OC leaders have risen to the challenges and opportunities provided by the OC movement.

We are already in the process of seeking God's discernment for the right people to make up the second batch of OC families (scheduled to begin training in spring 2017). We envision this batch as a place of opportunity for younger emerging leaders, and for singles as well as married couples.

As our OC groups continue to develop and minister, they will reach, baptize, disciple, mentor, and coach, finally releasing those they have reached to repeat the process. It is a model that is both biblical and true to the spirit of the original New Testament church. It also has the chance to be more relevant to educated urban dwellers than the current institutional church. Best of all, the OC will be able to survive and grow "under the radar," as intolerance and persecution continue to increase.

THE FUTURE:
IRRELEVANCE...THREAT...OR OPPORTUNITY?

CURRENT EVENTS IN my country (and I would suggest around the world) make it evident that times are changing. We are entering into a new era of intolerance, oppression, and persecution. As Christ followers, we must determine how we intend to lean into this future.

I would like to conclude this article with three observations that, while they each contain a warning, also offer us a glimpse of what God could have in store for us, and for a world starving for his love and grace:

- If the urban church is going to be relevant, we have to change our approach. The current approach of the institutional church is simply not working. In humility, I submit the Outreach Centre model as a way the church can regain its relevancy in the urban environment.

- If oppression, repression, and outright persecution continue to increase, we will have to detach ourselves from official, registered, "legal" church institutions, tied to large, identifiable buildings. To survive, we will have to go underground.

- But lest we lose sight of the big picture–the God picture, if you will–I believe God may be providing us a historic opportunity for dynamic vitality and growth of the Church. Over and over again, we have seen how persecution does not suppress, but rather sparks Christian growth. Examples like the Church in China, Nepal, and Vietnam are recent cases of this time-honored truth.

Yes, the Church in India could be in for tough times. It is possible that the Church universal could be in for tough times. And as humans, to feel fear and anxiety at times like these is natural. But as followers of Jesus, we can take comfort in the promises provided us by the Lord in the book of James:

> *Consider it pure joy, my brothers and sisters, whenever you face trials of many kinds, because you know that the testing of your faith produces perseverance. Let perseverance finish its work so that you may be mature and complete, not lacking anything....Blessed is the one who perseveres under trial because, having stood the test, that person will receive the crown of life that the Lord has promised to those who love him.*

> *James 1:2-4, 12*

Tea Time with the Police

Treating Your Oppressors as People

Editor's note: Because this leader lives and ministers in a country where repression and persecution of Christians is an issue, we have disguised this leader's identity and location.

"My supervisor has refused my request for leave, just as my wife was about to give birth." The man's chin trembled as he poured out his anxiety and grief.

He is a friend, a man I have spent much time with over the years. We have gotten to know and trust each other, to the point where he is willing to open up about his frustrations with his boss, his job, and even his purpose in life.

Yes, he is a friend...who is a member of the security police of my country. His job: to monitor Christians like me. Included in his duties: repressing the work of Christians, harassing men, women, and children guilty of nothing more than living as Christ followers, and breaking up entire house church networks.

I am one of his "cases." And yet, we are friends. How did this happen? And why have I been willing to bring this man and others like him into my circle of friends?

JOURNEY TO A MOST UNUSUAL AMBASSADORSHIP

AS A YOUNG MAN, I was a promising student. In the 1980s, I was permitted to move to the United States and begin PhD studies. I had been encouraged by my government to pursue doctoral studies in America.

But at the same time, I was active in a rising student movement advocating for more freedom and even democracy for our country. This movement was rising against a monolithic, one-party system that exercised control over virtually all aspects of our lives.

Our movement was not well received by those in power. Along with my fellow activists, I knew all of our activities were being monitored and recorded by our government. Still, we harbored increasing hope that things were changing for the better.

Those hopes were shattered in 1989 when the government brutally cracked down on a major student demonstration that had captured the world's attention for weeks. No one knows how many people were killed as army tanks rolled through our capitol city's central square, but it is said the death toll ran into the hundreds. Our budding democracy movement was effectively crushed. It was a devastating blow.

THE PARALLEL JOURNEY: CRISIS OF SPIRIT

AS OUR STUDENT movement was crumbling, it felt like equally heavy blows were raining down on my spirit. While

I was a person of privilege in my country, receiving a top university education and having the opportunity to pursue advanced studies in the West, I was the product of an atheistic educational system. I had no religion, no belief in any sort of God. Despite the elevated station I held in my society, I struggled with a sense of meaningless.

What was the point of it all? If this earthly life is the sum total of our existence, what did anything matter? My life felt like a train speeding into a dark tunnel–a tunnel taking me to the pit of spiritual despair.

It was then that I was given a gospel tract by a fellow student. I read the tract–and the impact on my spirit was nothing short of miraculous. There is a God! There is meaning in life! There is hope! I can have a real relationship with this God! I remember actually being scared by the joy that was flooding into my heart.

There, alone in my room, I knelt down and prayed a simple prayer. I became a Christ follower.

CHANGING PRIORITIES, CONSISTENT SYMPATHIES

IN 1993, MY WIFE and I were baptized. My priorities began to shift. I began to phase out of the political involvements that had previously dominated my life. But I remained sympathetic to the democracy movement that struggled to bring hope to a nation hiding its corruption behind a prosperous economy.

After I finished my PhD, I abandoned the secular career track and began theological studies at a Christian seminary. My goal was to return to my home country and share the gospel. I now had hope for my native land. There was an answer for my country–Jesus!

While I knew I wanted to return home to minister for Christ, I had no idea what ministry direction to pursue. But every time I prayed, three words would come to my mind: *students...campus...intellectuals.* I was getting a sense of my call–to reach out to the university students who had been part of my world for so long.

To do this, however, I felt I needed a legitimate platform with which to return to my country. I decided to take a job with a health food company in California. I worked there for two years as I prepared to return home. Then in 1999, I did return–as the chief representative for the California-based health food company. I was back home, with a valid business ID and a genuine business agenda. But along with my business career, I began to build relationships with university students in my free time. My vocation as a minister to students on campus had begun.

THE MINISTRY TAKES OFF

IT WAS AMAZING HOW easy it was at that time to lead students to Christ. There was a spiritual hunger and openness to the gospel that was palpable. Quickly, my ministry to students took off and grew rapidly.

People back in the West were hearing about what was happening spiritually in my country. They were excited with what they saw as an historical opportunity to reach the emerging generation of future leaders and influencers. Within a year, friends back in the United States approached me about providing financial support that would enable me to devote myself to student ministry full time.

I accepted their offer. Just that quickly, my vocation shifted–from businessperson to Christian campus minister. While I have retained my business license and still hold a position with the California health food company (albeit unpaid), beginning in 2000, my path was set toward Christian work. And just that quickly, my activities put me in the cross-hairs of my government.

TEA TIME WITH THE POLICE

WITHIN A FEW MONTHS, I received a visit. Two members of a government security agency came by to see me. (While the specific duties and powers of this agency are shaped by the agenda of our one-party, atheistic government, in structure they would be somewhat like America's FBI.) This agency was in charge of monitoring, investigating, controlling, and (when they chose to do so) dismantling religious activities like the Christian student outreach that I was doing.

It felt like my worst nightmares were coming to pass. While living in the West, I had heard horror stories about my government's persecution of the Christian house church movement–of believers being harassed, jailed, and martyred. And as I was preparing to return home in the late 1990s, I was harboring three deep fears:

- I would be kicked out of my country and deported back to the West.

- My children would be unable to survive the adjustment back home, especially the effects of the harsh educational system in our country.

- I would be placed under tight scrutiny, house arrest, or worse.

Now here it was–my first "tea time" with the religious police. The hammer was about to come down on me.

But what I did not yet realize is how, by 2000, things had changed. Twenty years before, in the turmoil of the 1980s, the security agencies had been populated with zealous believers of the ideology and supporters of the system. But by 2000, new, younger officers were on board. They did not share the zealotry of their predecessors. While they still supported the system, they saw themselves as professionals, assigned to do a job. Their interests revolved around career advancement and economic improvement.

Thus, "tea time." Two officers would visit: one to lead the conversation, the other to take notes. Rather than ugly interrogations, these were relatively civil and peaceful– monthly conversations over tea or drinks. But while the atmosphere was amicable, everyone knew what was behind these visits. They were very delicate encounters.

Many of my Christian brothers and sisters who also experienced visits like these saw "tea time" as one thing–a threat. They had no intention of engaging in any kind of conversation with their government monitors. Rather, they would stonewall. The only "conversation" they would offer were Bible verses and gospel presentations, which they would repeat again and again. The encounters were at best frigid; at worst, hostile.

EMPHATHIZING WITH THE ENEMY:
BUILDING FRIENDSHIPS WITH THE POLICE

I WAS INDEED frightened by these visits. My sense of vulnerability was acute. But for some reason, over time, a new thought began to grow in my mind: What if I treated the religious police officers as *people*? What if, rather than viewing these encounters as threats, I saw them as *part of my ministry*? What if, rather than being hostile or defensive, I tried to build bridges, develop authentic relationships, and even serve as a peacemaker of sorts?

This new perspective developed gradually, over time. And over the years, right up to today, my commitment to this approach is still mingled with fear. Part of me would love to never have another "tea time" with my police friends. But the conviction that God was calling me to treat the religious police as *real persons* grew and strengthened. And given the context of Scripture and the values of my country, it made sense.

Paul, in addressing the Corinthian church, identifies Christ followers as agents of reconciliation–to the point where we actually represent God as he reaches out with his message of love and grace:

> *All this is from God, who reconciled us to himself through*
> *Christ and gave us the ministry of reconciliation: that God*
> *was reconciling the world to himself in Christ, not counting*
> *people's sins against them. And he has committed to us the*
> *message of reconciliation. We are therefore Christ's ambassadors,*
> *as though God were making his appeal through us.*
>
> *2 Corinthians 5:18-20*

Paul also instructs the Corinthian believers to adapt themselves to their specific contexts, however difficult, in order to be able to reach others:

> *Though I am free and belong to no one, I have made myself*
> *a slave to everyone, to win as many as possible. To the Jews*
> *I became like a Jew, to win the Jews. To those under the law*
> *I became like one under the law (though I myself am not*
> *under the law), so as to win those under the law. To those not*
> *having the law I became like one not having the law (though*
> *I am not free from God's law but am under Christ's law), so*
> *as to win those not having the law. To the weak I became*
> *weak, to win the weak. I have become all things to all people*
> *so that by all possible means I might save some. I do all this*
> *for the sake of the gospel, that I may share in its blessings.*
>
> *1 Corinthians 9:19-23*

I could see that God wanted me to regard my police overseers not as enemies, not as objects, but as *people*. And I also knew that this perspective runs up against deep strains that permeate the culture of my country.

OUR CULTURAL HERITAGE: TREATING PERSONS AS OBJECTS

"YOUR COUNTRY IS FACING a humongous therapeutic challenge." I was in conversation with Dr. James Houston, known by many as the founding father at Regent College in Vancouver, Canada, where I had come for a period of additional study. We were discussing the state of my country as I prepared to return once again to my home.

Why was my country facing such a daunting challenge? "Because," he continued, "for generations, you were not treated as persons." He was spot on. For millennia, people in my country have been viewed as objects–tools to be used for some "greater" purpose:

- In the ancient value system that underpins the culture of my country, the person is an instrument for *family glory*.

- In the one-party system that currently rules our country, the person is an instrument for the *glory of the State*, or *the will of the Party*.

(Tragically, this same perspective has permeated many of our churches. In these churches, the person is an instrument for *church growth* and *ministry success*. However noble-sounding these goals might be, the people within these churches are not valued as people, but seen as tools. They are a means to an end.)

An additional dynamic of our culture added weight to my core convictions. For all of the rules and regulations that my government has on its books, my country is not ruled by laws, but by relationships. Our "laws" are constantly adjusted, manipulated, or ignored in favor of bonds of friendship and shared mutual interests.

The value of relationships over rules is a fundamental cultural truth for my country. So why couldn't this truth apply to my relationships with the police? Better yet, why not?

EASIER SAID THAN DONE

WHILE MY CONVICTIONS were strong, I knew this approach would be easier said than done. Historically, there has been icy hostility between the government and the Christian house church movement of which I was a part. Many, if not most, of my Christian brothers and sisters viewed government officials as vicious, satanic–in short, the enemy. As I have mentioned, they would refuse to relate to government officials at all unless absolutely forced to; and when forced, they would resort to the sanctuary of Bible verses and scripted gospel presentations.

The religious structures in my country posed an additional layer of difficulty. As in other countries where there is religious oppression, my country has both officially sanctioned (registered) churches and unsanctioned, technically illegal (unregistered) churches. There is deep mistrust between these two groups. Registered church leaders view the unregistered churches as law-flouting renegades, ignoring government order. Unregistered church leaders view the registered church as collaborators, their ranks riddled with government informers.

So the challenge before me was not only to be a peacemaker between the church and the government, but also between the conflicting branches of the church itself. But I knew my willingness to engage with my government monitors would cause me to be viewed with suspicion by both sides. I had to commit to a path that would somehow enable me to navigate shark-infested waters.

BRIDGES—WITH BOUNDARIES

AT THE NEXT VISIT with my government monitors, I cleared the air regarding my perspective on our relationship— and outlined the boundaries I had determined would be needed if our relationship was to succeed.

"I am a Christian," I told them. "And I am also a patriot. While I may have a different perspective on patriotism than yours, I love my country. And I want to not just have surface conversations—I want us to get to know one another.

"But you need to know that there are things I will never give you. I will never give you names, numbers, or any other specific information on the activities of my Christian brothers and sisters. In short, I will not be an informer. All these 'secrets' I believe you can easily uncover without my assistance. Frankly, if the feeble efforts of my Christian friends to maintain secrecy can hide us from your radar, then I'm worried about our national security." (This was my attempt at a joke.)

"What I will provide you is my perspective as a Christian on information you already have. In a sense, you can consider me a consultant. My goal is to help you better understand the Christian movement you purport to investigate and monitor, and to help you gain a right context on the Bible, Christian theology, church history, American culture, and other relevant issues.

"I look forward to our conversations. But I must ask you to respect my privacy."

Even as I laid out my hopes for the relationship, I knew we had a long way to go. We have a saying in our language: *Ice three feet thick is not formed overnight*. It had taken time for the barriers between Christians and our government to be built; it would take time for these barriers to be lowered.

PROGRESS AND PUSHBACK

AS I HAVE mentioned, police visits are usually done in pairs. But after some time, the note-taker stopped coming, while his supervisor continued to meet with me one on one. This man continued to try to gather information for his reports, but we began to spend more and more time in non-report-related conversation. We would have drinks, chat, and share. Little by little, we were becoming friends.

Over time, he began to disclose more and more about his life and the struggles he was facing (such as the time when he was denied leave to be with his wife when she was due to give birth). He even began to express doubts about his profession. Now understand that this man had already experienced quite a bit of success in his work. Within three years of his graduation from police school, he had uncovered and dismantled an entire house church network. He received awards for his accomplishment and was considered an up-and-comer in his department.

But his "success" was eating at him. "Dr. ‒‒," he told me, "I don't think I'm doing the right job. I was trained to fight criminals. But for the past three years I have been making trouble for little girls, old men and women, the weak and the vulnerable in our country. I am harassing people I should be protecting, just because they are Christians. Why am I doing this?"

I began to realize how pitifully little this man and his colleagues actually knew about Christians and Christianity, and how warped their perceptions were. I learned that in police school, the entire extent of the "training" on Christianity this man and his colleagues had received was the viewing of a propaganda film that purported to show Catholic nuns using abandoned children for diabolical medical experiments–after which they buried the bodies in church courtyards!

My friend also became more and more aware of his appalling lack of knowledge. One day, he startled me with a request: "Dr. ––, you should come and do seminars on Christianity for our police officers."

We continued to get to know each other. As our friendship grew, we developed mutual sympathies. We became aware that we are all human, struggling in twisted systems. Our systems are just twisted in different ways. And I began to realize that police officers like my friend were some of the most abused people in our twisted government system. They were victims as much as predators.

But while I was encouraged by the relationship I was building with my police friend, I faced strong criticism from many of my Christian friends. They were deeply skeptical of any possibility that a legitimate relationship could be developed with an agent of the government. "You are being used," they would say. "He is just taking advantage of you. Someday, you are going to regret this."

OPPRESSOR OUTREACH: NO PREACHING, NO PROBLEM

A MAJOR ISSUE I faced as I developed this relationship was evangelism. Would I share the gospel with my friend? If so, how should I share it?

I have mentioned that typical Christian/police encounters in my country often became evangelistic encounters... of a sort. The Christians would quote Bible verses and preach gospel presentations. Many police became quite familiar with–if not actually impacted by–a handful of Scripture verses and standard gospel presentations.

For whatever reason, I never preached to this man. I did not present gospel outlines. Rather, I tried to relate to him as a friend and as a Christ follower trying to live as an ambassador for my Lord.

My connection with this man was really God's timing. We met just as he had completed his successful dismantling of the house church network. In the process, he had come to genuinely want to know more about Christianity. But he became more and more frustrated as the only "conversations" he seemed to have with the Christians he encountered became recitations of Bible verses and core doctrines.

This policeman was part of a huge system, full of people like himself whose job it was to monitor and suppress Christianity. But these same people did not actually know any Christians personally. He wanted to make friends with a Christian. That turned out to be me.

Our conversations were not evangelistic. But they were fruitful. One day over tea, he told me, "Dr. – –, you haven't evangelized me. But somehow, I feel like every sentence from your mouth is like the gospel." Somehow, God was using our wide-ranging conversations, and the sharing of our lives, to get his truth through to this man.

I would love to tell you my friend has become a believer, but I cannot. He is not yet a Christian, but we are still friends. It is a relationship we both want to continue–even though we no longer have to. You see, I am no longer part of his caseload.

PRESENT DAY: TRUST—WITH LIMITS

TODAY, I STILL ENJOY my ongoing friendship with this police officer. And several years ago, my network doubled. In 2007, a field officer from a more powerful government security agency also began to visit with me. (The closest US equivalent to the agency this man represented would be the CIA.)

In the same way as with my first friend, I have, slowly and over time, built a relationship and friendship with this man. And like my first friend, he shares an acute lack of knowledge about–and a genuine interest in–Christianity. I was not surprised when he asked me one day, "Dr.––, could you spend time with me and my colleagues? As religious officers, we understand woefully little about Christianity, and our superiors understand even less."

He is quite correct. And the trickle of information today's religious police receive on Christianity has a new perverted twist. Unlike their predecessors, who were taught that our faith was little more than superstition and human sacrifice, they are now being told that Christianity is a rising threat to the security of our country.

Even though I still struggle with fear as I engage in these relationships, I choose to continue them. I choose to trust these men–with limits. After all, they are working for a repressive, atheistic government. They have an agenda. In every conversation I have with them, I am praying all the while for God to give me strength, wisdom, and discernment.

As I look back, I can see that my building of these relationships was not so much a conscious choice, but a gradual process. I was almost dragged into these situations. But over time, I came to understand that God put me into these relationships for a reason. And while it still remains a struggle, and still remains a process, I am thankful for the bridge-building, peacemaking opportunities God has given me.

The fundamental principle remains—my understanding of what it means to be an ambassador for Christ. It is about building relationships with whomever God chooses to bring across our path. And even when the relationship is as fraught with peril as a friendship between a Christian and a member of an oppressive government's religious police, Scripture tells us that, in these moments of connection, Christ is choosing to make his case through us.

Anxieties notwithstanding...fears notwithstanding... these relationships are not a threat. They are part of my ministry.

About the Authors

DAVID DAYALAN is pastor of Gurgaon Christian Fellowship in Gurgaon, Haryana, India. He also serves as national director for Asian Access India and as A2's Vice President for Program Development. He, his wife Anita, and their youngest daughter Sianna live in Gurgaon.

ADRIAN DeVISSER is founder and senior pastor of Kethu Sevana Ministries in Sri Lanka. He also serves as national director for Asian Access Sri Lanka as well as A2's Vice President for Partnership Development. He and his wife Ophelia live in Colombo, Sri Lanka.

JEYAKARAN EMMANUEL is founding pastor of Powerhouse Church in Chennai, Tamil Nadu, India. He also serves as South India Coordinator for Asian Access India. He, his wife Kavitha, and their daughter Abigail Ritika live in Chennai.

KAVITHA EMMANUEL is founder of *Women of Worth*. She is also co-pastor of Powerhouse Church.

YOSHIYA HARI is pastor of Saikyo Hope Chapel as well as national director of Asian Access Japan. He, his wife Megumi, their son Akito and their daughter Kaori live in Toda Saitama, Japan.

MENG AUN HOUR is founder and senior pastor of Followers of Jesus Church in Phnom Penh, Cambodia, as well as president of United Pastors Fellowship. He also serves as national director for Asian Access Cambodia. He, his wife Rady, and their daughter Vouchly live in Phnom Penh.

ALMA KYAWTHURA is pastor of New Life in Christ Ministries, based in Yangon, Myanmar. She lives in North Dagon Township, Yangon, with her husband Wesley, their son Trust, and their daughter Phobe.

WESLEY KYAWTHURA is national director for Asian Access Myanmar.

PETER DEBAKAR MAZUMDER serves as national director of Bible Students Fellowship in Bangladesh as well as co-national director of Asian Access Bangladesh. He lives in Dhaka, Bangladesh with his wife Sylvia and their daughters Parmina and Joanna.

LEOR P. SARKAR is general secretary of Bangladesh Baptist Church Fellowship as well as co-national director of Asian Access Bangladesh. He lives in Dhaka, Bangladesh with his wife Panna, daughter Prachi, and son Propat.

TAKESHI TAKAZAWA has been involved in leader development and church multiplication with Asian Access since 1989. He and his wife Dorrie live in Tokyo, Japan.

About Asian Access

*Asian Access is a vibrant community
devoted to helping leaders thrive*

We are a leader development group that identifies and develops
the right leaders at the right time through the right process,
so they can be released to make the greatest Kingdom impact
across Asia.

Asian Access (A2) sustains change through a proven process that
takes the region's most promising leaders and equips them to
have a disproportionately significant impact in their countries,
cultures and continent. We want every leader to:

- Live in a love relationship with God.
- Grow as a Christ-like leader.
- Reproduce disciple-making leaders.
- Catalyze reproducible movements.

Changing the few who change the many

Our focus is on intentionally training a few key leaders at a time,
through a two-year transformational process, so they can lead
the church with vision, character and competence. Our community of leaders extends across eleven countries with vision to
reach twenty countries of Asia, striving to unite the church,
extend the Kingdom, and transform the cultures of Asia for the
glory of God.

www.asianaccess.org
www.asianaccess.biz
info@asianaccess.org

58975796R00178

Made in the USA
San Bernardino, CA
01 December 2017